Here's all the great literature in this grade level of *Celebrate Reading!*

"Mom, Mom, My Ears Are Growing!"

And Other Joys of the Real World

Bingo Brown, Gypsy Lover
from the novel by
Betsy Byars
✹ *School Library Journal*
Best Book
✹ ALA Notable Children's Book

The Cybil War
from the novel by
Betsy Byars
✹ ALA Notable Children's Book
✹ Children's Choice

Remarkable Children
from the book by
Dennis Brindell Fradin

And Still I Rise
from the collection by
Maya Angelou
✹ *School Library Journal*
Best Book

How It Feels to Fight for Your Life
from the book by
Jill Krementz
✹ Outstanding Science
Trade Book
✹ Teachers' Choice

Fast Sam, Cool Clyde, and Stuff
from the novel by
Walter Dean Myers
✹ Children's Choice

The Summer of the Falcon
from the novel by
Jean Craighead George
✹ Newbery Medal Author

Featured Poet
Maya Angelou

BOOK B

Look Both Ways

Seeing the Other Side

Free to Fly
A User's Guide to the Imagination

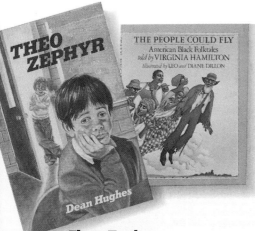

Featured Poets
Paul Fleischman
Pat Mora
Shel Silverstein
Jane Yolen
Judith Viorst

Journey Home

and Other Routes to Belonging

Featured Poets
Gwendolyn Brooks
Edwin Muir

Arriving Before I Start

Passages Through Time

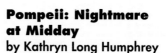

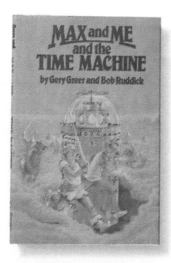

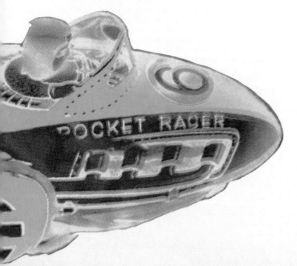

Just Like a Hero

Talk About Leadership

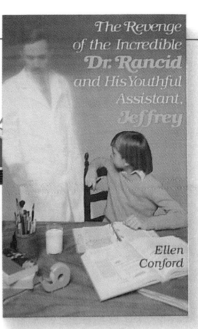

The Revenge of the Incredible Dr. Rancid and His Youthful Assistant, Jeffrey
from the novel by
Ellen Conford
✹ Young Readers' Choice
Award Author

The Gold Coin
by Alma Flor Ada
✹ Christopher Award

Mother Teresa
from the biography by
Patricia Reilly Giff

Prince of the Double Axe
by Madeleine Polland

Featured Poet
John Greenleaf Whittier

Celebrate Reading!
Trade Book Library

Our Sixth-Grade Sugar Babies
by Eve Bunting
* *School Library Journal* Best Book

Goodbye, Chicken Little
by Betsy Byars
* Children's Choice
* Children's Editors' Choice
* Library of Congress Children's Book
* *New York Times* Notable Book

Dragon of the Lost Sea
by Laurence Yep
* ALA Notable Children's Book
* International Reading Association 100 Favorite Paperbacks of 1989

The Westing Game
by Ellen Raskin
* Newbery Medal
* Boston Globe-Horn Book Award

The Brocaded Slipper and Other Vietnamese Tales
by Lynette Vuong

The Jedera Adventure
by Lloyd Alexander
* Parents' Choice

The Endless Steppe: Growing Up in Siberia
by Esther Hautzig
* ALA Notable Children's Book
* Boston Globe-Horn Book Award Honor Book
* Lewis Carroll Shelf Award

Baseball in April and Other Stories
by Gary Soto
* ALA Notable Children's Book
* *Parenting* Reading-Magic Award

Tom's Midnight Garden
by Philippa Pearce
* Carnegie Medal Winner

The House of Dies Drear
by Virginia Hamilton
* ALA Notable Children's Book

Journey to Jo'burg: A South African Story
by Beverly Naidoo
* Notable Social Studies Trade Book

Jackie Joyner-Kersee
by Neil Cohen

Titles in This Set

About the Cover Artist
Ron Villani enjoys drawing in a comic-book style. As a boy he started
collecting comic books, not for the stories or the characters, but
because he had favorite comic-book artists. He has a large collection
and is often asked to paint in the style of particular comic-book artists.

ISBN 0-673-82121-8

1995 printing
Copyright © 1993
Scott, Foresman and Company, Glenview, Illinois
All Rights Reserved.
Printed in the United States of America.

Acknowledgments appear on page 144.

2345678910RRS9998979695

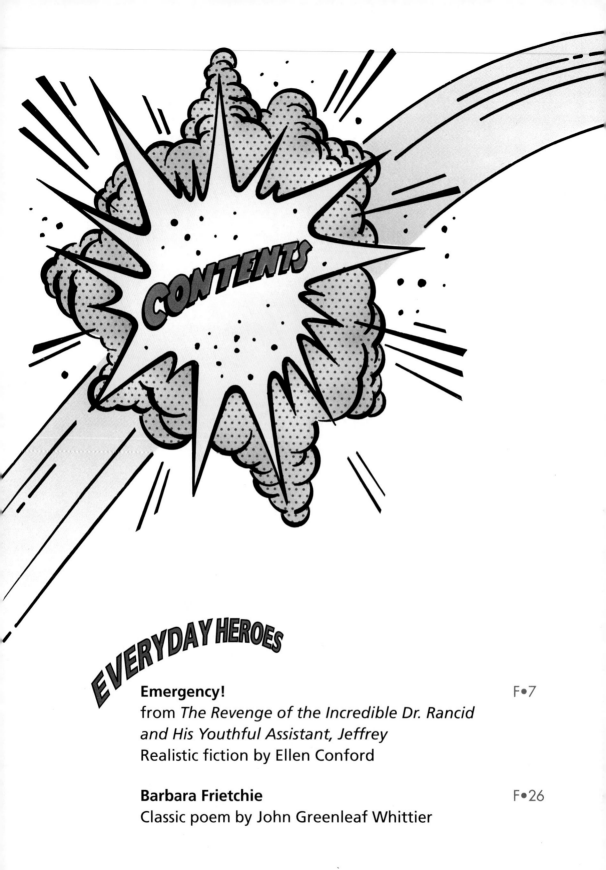

CONTENTS

EVERYDAY HEROES

EMERGENCY!

from *The Revenge of the Incredible Dr. Rancid and His Youthful Assistant, Jeffrey*

by Ellen Conford

The phone raaaaaaaaang.

"Oh, Jeffie, thank goodness you're home!"

"Mrs. Winchell?" Mrs. Winchell is Matthew, Mark, and Fletcher's mother.

"Listen, Jeff, this is an emergency. My husband won't be in till six and our regular baby-sitter has a stomach virus and no one in the world seems to be home and I have my midterm abnormal psychology exam in *half an hour*—"

"You want me to stay with the kids?"

"Oh, please, Jeffie, if you can. I'll pay you—I should have left by now—"

"No problem. I'll be right over. And you don't have to pay me."

"We'll talk about that later. Just come!"

"On my way."

I hung up the phone, grabbed my jacket from the closet, and ran out the front door and down the steps. It was four o'clock and my mother had left a note saying she'd be late and we'd go out to eat when she got home.

It was raining lightly when I got to the Winchells' house down the block, and Mrs. Winchell was standing at the door, holding it open for me.

"You're a lifesaver, honey," she said. "I'll only be two hours, but Dave should be home first and you can leave when he gets here." Dave is her husband.

"Don't worry about it," I said. She really looked frantic. She often does, but not usually this frantic.

Mrs. Winchell is going to college, and between her three kids and classes and the house, she's probably got her hands full.

"Don't worry about a thing," I said. "Good luck on your exam."

"Thanks, dear." She patted the air near my head—I think she meant to pat me on the head, but she was in a hurry. She waved to Matthew, Mark, and Fletcher, who were lined up in the hall behind her. "Be good for Jeff, now, boys." She ran out the door.

I'd never actually baby-sat for the Winchell kids before, but I played with them and Bix occasionally, so I really didn't think there'd be any problems. They're good kids and young enough to look up to me as one of the "big kids."

Matthew is eight, Mark is six, and Fletcher is four. They look a lot alike, all with straight blond hair and blue eyes. Standing there lined up in size place, they were really sort of cute.

I herded them into the family room and we sat down in a circle on the floor.

"Okay, men," I said briskly, "what'll we do? Who wants to watch TV?"

"Me!" yelled Fletcher,

as if he hardly ever got the chance to watch TV.

"Let's play basketball," Matthew said.

"No, it's raining out. It's no good playing in the rain."

"I want to play Uncle Wiggily," said Mark.

"Isn't there something you all like to do?" I asked.

They looked at each other thoughtfully. Matthew's eyes lit up.

"Yeah! Make concoctions."

"Yeah! Coctions!" Fletcher yelled.

Mark nodded. "We all like that."

"What's making concoctions?" I asked.

Matthew smiled happily. "We go into the bathroom and mix up a whole lot of things from the medicine cabinet and add some food coloring or paint or something and maybe some soap so it bubbles."

"Then what do you do with it?" I asked nervously.

Matthew shrugged. "Usually flush it down the toilet. Unless we wanted to kill somebody. Then we'd try to get him to drink it."

"I don't think your mother would like that too much."

"That's why we should do it now," Matthew said.

Very logical.

"No concoctions," I said sternly.

"Now, what else do you all like to do?"

"Watch 'The Flintstones'!" yelled Fletcher.

"Play Uncle Wiggily," Mark insisted.

"Make a cake," said Matthew.

That didn't sound like a bad idea. If Mrs. Winchell had any cake mix around, it should be pretty easy, and think how pleased she'd be when she came back to find a nice, homemade cake waiting for her.

"I'll tell you what. We'll mix up the cake and then, while it's baking, we'll play Uncle Wiggily. How's that, Mark?"

Mark thought about it for a minute. "Okay."

"Come on, Fletcher. We're going to make a cake and then play Uncle Wiggily."

"Don't know how to make a cake," said Fletcher. He turned on the television and plopped down on his huge stuffed turtle in front of the screen.

"'The Flintstones'!"

he yelled. "'The Flintstones' is on!" He bounced up and down on his turtle.

"Oh, let him watch," Matthew said. "He'd just be in the way anyhow."

"Okay, you watch 'The Flintstones,' but *don't* move. Okay, Fletcher?"

Fletcher was staring at the set. He didn't look like he'd ever move.

"Don't worry," said Matthew. "He'd stay there all night if you let him."

We went into the kitchen and Matthew found a box of cake mix. He got out a bowl and the eggs. The electric mixer was right on the counter, and both Matthew and Mark insisted they knew how to use it.

They each got to break one egg into the bowl.

We were picking eggshells out of the cake mix when there was a horrible scream from the family room.

I raced in there and found Fletcher holding his mouth and crying.

"Fletcher, what happened?" I grabbed his hand away from his mouth. I thought my heart was going to stop. He was bleeding like a stuck pig. Blood seemed to be gushing out of his mouth, down his chin.

"Oh, my God! Fletcher,

what happened? What did you do?" He just kept screaming and crying.

I was panic-stricken. How much could a little kid like that bleed before he lost too much blood? And how had he hurt himself so badly? And what was I going to do? My mother wasn't home, and Mrs. Winchell said *nobody* was home—

"Matthew," I said, trying to sound calm, except that my voice was shaking, "get me one of your father's clean handkerchiefs."

Matthew ran upstairs and was back down again in a minute with a handkerchief. I tried to press it against Fletcher's lip, but he twisted around and screamed right through the handkerchief.

"It's okay, Fletcher," I said. "It's okay. This'll make it better."

But it didn't. He seemed to bleed even more.

I picked him up. I remembered that three blocks away, on Staunton Road, there was a house with a doctor's name sign on the front. We don't go to him but it was close and at the moment, that was the only thing I could think of to do.

"You two, get your raincoats and umbrellas if you have them. Hurry up; we're taking Fletcher to the doctor."

"What doctor?" asked Mark.

"Move it!" I yelled.

"Get Fletcher's coat too."

They ran. Even Mark didn't dawdle.

My heart pounding, I carried Fletcher into the kitchen. I washed off the handkerchief and put it against his lips again. He was only crying now, not screaming anymore.

There was a blackboard in the kitchen with *Yogurt, milk, coffee, granola,* written on it. I wrote under that, *I took Fletcher to the doctor. Don't worry. Jeff.* If Mr. or Mrs. Winchell got back before we did and saw the blood on the floor in the family room and kitchen, at least they'd know I had the situation under control.

Sure I did. I was shaking so hard I could have homogenized Fletcher.

Matthew and Mark were back in an instant. We put Fletcher's coat and hat on and ran down the front steps.

It was raining much harder now.

"You guys walk under the umbrella," I said, "and let's go."

e jogged the three blocks to the doctor's. Fletcher is not a particularly heavy kid, but neither am I, so by the time we reached the door my arms were aching. I rang the bell and walked in.

The waiting room was full of people. I staggered up to the nurse at the desk and gasped, "Emergency. *Please.*" She looked at the four of us. Mark was holding the open umbrella and dripping all over the carpet.

"What kind of emergency?"

I held out the bloody handkerchief for her to see.

"All right, take a seat please. I'll have the doctor see him right away."

We didn't take a seat. We just stood there. She went somewhere down a hall and came back a few minutes later.

"Come with me, please." I followed her, and Matthew and Mark followed me.

"You boys," she said, "wait out there, all right?"

"He's my brother," Matthew said.

"Don't worry. We'll take good care of him. Just wait in the reception room."

"Go on," I told Matthew. "You watch Mark."

I carried Fletcher down the hall. The nurse led me into a small room with an examining table. "Just put him down there," she said.

Fletcher looked around. He must have finally realized he was in a doctor's office, because he began to wail.

"No shots! No shots!"

The bleeding didn't look so bad now, but his chin and mouth were a mess of red smears.

A real tall guy in a white coat came into the room. Except for the white coat, he looked more like a football player than a doctor.

"Is this the patient?" he asked pleasantly, putting his hand on Fletcher's head.

"No shots!" yelled Fletcher.

"No shots!"

"Well." The doctor smiled. "He sounds in pretty good shape."

"This really was an emergency," I said. I didn't want the doctor to think I shouldn't have bothered him. "I was baby-sitting with him and all of a sudden he yelled and he was bleeding all over the rug. His mouth."

"Yes. Open your mouth, son."

"No shots!" Fletcher yelled. The doctor ducked his head down and grabbed a peek at Fletcher's mouth.

"What happened to him?"

"I don't know," I said miserably. "We were making a cake. He was in the other room watching television. I shouldn't have left him alone."

"Let's get this cleaned up and take a look. Why don't you wait outside?"

"He's just a little kid. He'll be scared."

The door opened and another nurse walked in. "Not with Jeannie here," the doctor said. He looked at Fletcher. "You're not scared, are you?" Fletcher looked at Jeannie.

Jeannie smiled. "And what's *your* name?"

"No shots," Fletcher said, but more quietly now.

"What a nice name, No Shots. What's your last name, No Shots?"

Fletcher giggled.

I was so relieved, I left him there with the doctor and Jeannie and went into the waiting room.

Matthew and Mark were sitting in the middle of the reception-room floor, their slickers still dripping little puddles around them. The umbrella was open and Mark was twirling it upside down in front of him, like a top.

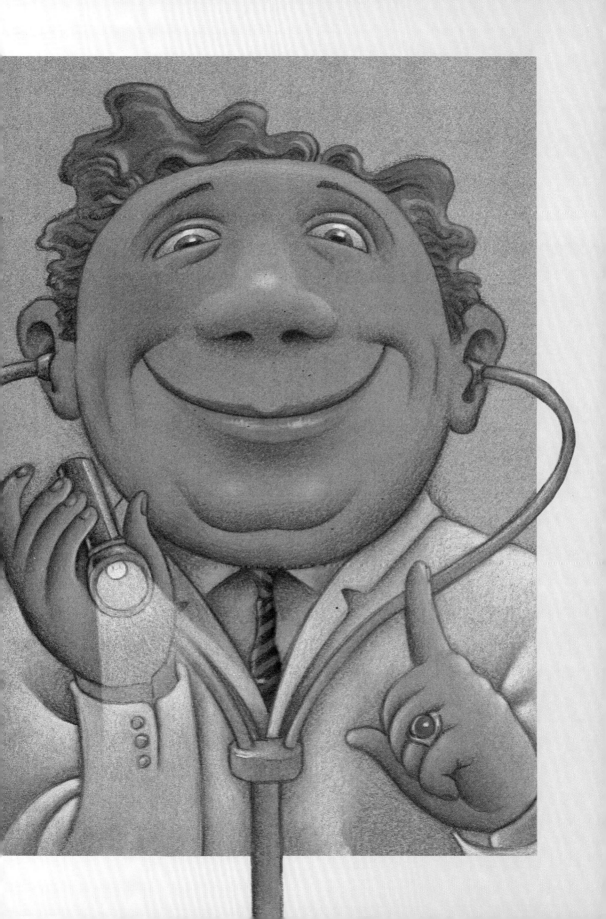

"He'll be okay," I said. "The doctor's taking care of him. Close the umbrella, Mark."

"I don't know how."

Matthew reached for it and closed it. "Did they find out why he was bleeding like that?"

I shook my head. "No, but the doctor'll take care of him."

I slumped down into a chair and tried not to show the boys how upset I was. I didn't know what the doctor would have to do to Fletcher, but whatever it was, I knew it was my fault for leaving him alone. How would I ever explain this to Mrs. Winchell?

The nurse at the desk called me over. "I'll need some information about him. He's not a patient of ours, is he?"

"I don't think so. I'm his baby-sitter. Those are his brothers."

Some baby-sitter, I thought. She was probably thinking the same thing.

I gave Fletcher's name and age, and Matthew gave the nurse his parents' names and their address and telephone number.

"Do you have any relatives in the vicinity?" she asked Matthew. He looked at her blankly.

"Does any of your family live around here?" I asked him.

"My mother and father," he said.

"Besides them."

He shook his head.

I began to get even more worried. "You mean, next of kin?" Why did they need to know the next of kin? That was what you had to know when someone was *dying.*

"Is it that serious?"

I tried to keep my voice down so as not to worry the kids, but my heart began to pound like a hammer. I thought I would keel over before she said, "Of course not. We just like to know if there's an adult relative to sign forms and things if necessary."

"Why would it be necessary?" My voice shook.

But before she could answer, Fletcher came trotting down the hall, one hand in Jeannie's, proudly waving a wooden tongue depressor.

"He's fine!" the nurse said. "And he was so brave. Weren't you brave, No Shots?"

Fletcher laughed delightedly.

"The doctor wants to see you for a minute." She pointed down the hall.

I practically ran down the hall and found the doctor washing up in the little room where Fletcher had been.

"What happened?" I asked breathlessly. "What did you have to do? Is he okay?"

"He's fine. All it was, really, was a cut upper lip. It looked a lot worse than it was. You know, those mouth and lip cuts bleed like crazy. They scare the heck out of most parents."

I breathed a loud sigh of relief and slumped against the wall. "He doesn't need stitches or anything?"

"I don't think so. I didn't want to do anything too much without his parents here. The bleeding is stopped, so it ought to be okay."

"Did you find out how it happened?"

"The nearest I could figure out," the doctor said, drying his hands, "is that he got into a fight with a turtle."

"Ohh. He must have been wrestling with his stuffed turtle."

"Then he probably just bit his lip hard. But since we don't know for sure, tell his parents to call me. If he's not up-to-date on his shots, his own doctor should give him a tetanus shot. You be sure and have them call me when they get home, all right?"

"All right," I said. "Thanks a lot."

I went back into the waiting room. Fletcher was standing on a chair, waving his tongue depressor around like a symphony conductor.

"Let's go, guys. Come on, Fletcher, we'll get your coat and hat on."

"No Shots," said Fletcher. He jumped up and down on the chair. "Name is No Shots."

I grabbed him and got his coat on. "No jumping, No Shots. No jumping, no running, no turtle wrestling."

Three people in the waiting room tittered.

Very funny.

It wasn't until we trudged back to the Winchells' house that I realized that I had no key and we'd locked ourselves out. So we went to my house and Matthew kept watch at the front window till he saw his father's car pull into their driveway.

My stomach jerked crazily. I was not looking forward to explaining this.

I got Fletcher's slicker back on, and we went down the block to the Winchells'. Mr. Winchell had just opened the front door when we reached the house.

"Hey, what's up, kids? What are you doing out in this rain?" Fletcher waved his tongue depressor as he trotted into the house. "My turtle bit me and I was bleeding and the doctor gave me this because I was so brave."

"what?"

My heart sinking into my stomach, I explained.

Mr. Winchell looked stunned for a moment. Then he bent down in front of Fletcher. "Let's see where your turtle bit you."

Fletcher opened his mouth.

"Oh, that doesn't look so bad," he said.

"It was bad," said Fletcher. "It was very bad. I was *bleeding*. It *hurt*. Is 'The Flintstones' on?" Still wearing his raincoat, he wandered off into the family room.

"I'm really sorry, Mr. Winchell. I left him alone in there and I shouldn't have. It's all my fault."

"Jeff, I'm very grateful you were here. You can't watch him every minute. Good grief, he's in there alone half the day. This could have happened anytime. You were terrific, the way you handled the whole thing. You should be very proud of yourself."

I shook my head. I think he was just being nice. There wouldn't have been anything to handle if I had kept my eye on Fletcher.

I gave him the doctor's card, which the nurse had given me before we left the office.

"I'd better go call him. Listen, Jeff, thanks a million. Thanks for *everything*."

"Sure. So long, Matthew. So long, Mark."

"Bye, Jeff," said Matthew. Mark didn't say anything for a minute. Then, as I was halfway out the door, he called, "Jeff? You promised to play Uncle Wiggily."

I was still feeling pretty upset when my parents got home, and even dinner out at Cliff's Shore Manor didn't do a thing to make me feel better.

My parents kept asking me why I was in such a bad mood, but I didn't want to tell them. I was somehow hoping they'd never find out about the whole thing. I could imagine how proud of me they'd be if they knew that while I was supposed to be responsible for the Winchell kids I had let one of them practically bleed to death.

A few minutes after we got back from the restaurant, the doorbell rang.

My father went to open it and there was Mrs. Winchell, her hair damp and frizzing, not even wearing a raincoat. She was breathless.

"Oh, Jeff!" She headed right for me. "Liz, Spence, did you hear what happened? Did you hear what Jeff did?"

I wanted to shrink into the walls before she could grab me—I thought she might want to clout me a good one in the head. I was stunned when she grabbed me and hugged me so hard I couldn't breathe for a minute.

Then she told them the whole thing—very dramatically.

"Jeff, you were just—just—" She grabbed me and hugged me again. "You should be proud of this boy," she said to my mother. "He saved the day. I don't know what would have happened if he wasn't there."

I was getting more and more embarrassed by the minute. When she pressed some bills into my hand, I cringed.

"*No!*" I tried to hand them back but she wouldn't take them.

"Please, Mrs. Winchell, I don't want any money. I'm just sorry that Fletcher got hurt when I was supposed to be watching him."

"Are you crazy, Jeffie? He gets hurt while *I'm* watching him. If I felt guilty every time one of those three got a cut or a bruise, I'd be in a rubber room by now. And you keep that money. It's not nearly enough for what you did. You just better know how grateful we are, that's all."

My parents were standing there looking dazed as she let herself out the front door.

"Why didn't you tell us?"

"Jeff, I'm so proud of you," my mother said.

"You really come through in an emergency." My father was beaming at me, as if I had won the 100-yard dash, or something.

What was the matter with everybody? Why couldn't they see what I saw? I had loused things up again, and everyone was praising me like I was some kind of hero or something.

I stuffed the money Mrs. Winchell had forced on me into a pocket. "It was my fault in the first place," I muttered. "Nothing to be proud of."

But they kept beaming at me and carrying on about it for the whole rest of the evening, so that by the time I went to bed, I was beginning to let myself feel just the tiniest little bit like a hero.

THINKING ABOUT IT

1

"You saved the day." When has someone said that to you, and why? When *should* someone have said that to you, and why?

2

This story is from a book entitled *The Revenge of the Incredible Dr. Rancid and His Youthful Assistant, Jeffrey.* What in the world does one have to do with the other? What might the book's plot be about if this is one incident in it?

3

A new story! It is not a medical emergency that happens while Jeffrey is baby-sitting for Matthew, Mark, and Fletcher. It is a funny problem or emergency that arises while they are baking the cake. Tell the new story.

BARBARA FRIETCHIE

★ ★ ★ ★ ★

BY JOHN GREENLEAF WHITTIER

Up from the meadows rich with corn,
Clear in the cool September morn,

The clustered spires of Frederick stand
Green-walled by the hills of Maryland.

Round about them orchards sweep,
Apple and peach tree fruited deep,

Fair as the garden of the Lord
To the eyes of the famished rebel horde,

On that pleasant morn of the early fall
When Lee marched over the mountain-wall;

Over the mountains winding down,
Horse and foot, into Frederick town.

Forty flags with their silver stars,
Forty flags with their crimson bars,

Flapped in the morning wind: the sun
Of noon looked down, and saw not one.

Up rose old Barbara Frietchie then,
Bowed with her fourscore years and ten;

Bravest of all in Frederick town,
She took up the flag the men hauled down;

In her attic window the staff she set,
To show that one heart was loyal yet.

Up the street came the rebel tread,
Stonewall Jackson riding ahead.

Under his slouched hat left and right
He glanced; the old flag met his sight.

"Halt!"—the dust-brown ranks stood fast.
"Fire!"—out blazed the rifle-blast.

It shivered the window, pane and sash;
It rent the banner with seam and gash.

Quick as it fell, from the broken staff
Dame Barbara snatched the silken scarf.

She leaned far out on the windowsill,
And shook it forth with a royal will.

"Shoot, if you must, this old gray head,
But spare your country's flag," she said.

A shade of sadness, a blush of shame,
Over the face of the leader came;

The nobler nature within him stirred
To life at that woman's deed and word;

"Who touches a hair of yon gray head
Dies like a dog! March on!" he said.

All day long through the Frederick street
Sounded the tread of marching feet:

All day long that free flag tossed
Over the heads of the rebel host.

Ever its torn folds rose and fell
On the loyal winds that loved it well;

And through the hill-gaps sunset light
Shone over it with a warm good-night.

Barbara Frietchie's work is o'er,
And the Rebel rides on his raids no more.

Honor to her! and let a tear
Fall, for her sake, on Stonewall's bier.

Over Barbara Frietchie's grave,
Flag of Freedom and Union wave!

Peace and order and beauty draw
Round thy symbol of light and law;

And ever the stars above look down
On thy stars below in Frederick town!

THINKING ABOUT IT

1

You are perhaps the ten millionth person to read this poem. If ten million people read a poem, it must have something. What is it?

2

This poem contains a famous quote. What is it? What other famous quotes do you know?

3

This poem has rhyme and rhythm. How will you use rhyme and rhythm and other qualities in the poem to make it interesting as you perform it for others to hear?

THE GOLD COIN

by Alma Flor Ada

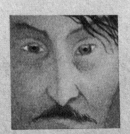

Juan had been a thief for many years. Because he did his stealing by night, his skin had become pale and sickly. Because he spent his time either hiding or sneaking about, his body had become shriveled and bent. And because he had neither friend nor relative to make him smile, his face was always twisted into an angry frown.

One night, drawn by a light shining through the trees, Juan came upon a hut. He crept up to the door and through a crack saw an old woman sitting at a plain, wooden table.

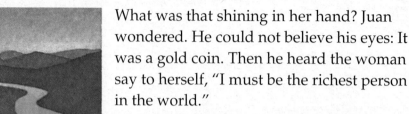

What was that shining in her hand? Juan wondered. He could not believe his eyes: It was a gold coin. Then he heard the woman say to herself, "I must be the richest person in the world."

Juan decided instantly that all the woman's gold must be his. He thought that the easiest thing to do was to watch until the woman left. Juan hid in the bushes and huddled under his poncho, waiting for the right moment to enter the hut.

Juan was half asleep when he heard knocking at the door and the sound of insistent voices. A few minutes later, he saw the woman, wrapped in a black cloak, leave the hut with two men at her side.

Here's my chance! Juan thought. And, forcing open a window, he climbed into the empty hut.

He looked about eagerly for the gold. He looked under the bed. It wasn't there. He looked in the cupboard. It wasn't there, either. Where could it be? Close to despair, Juan tore away some beams supporting the thatch roof.

Finally, he gave up. There was simply no gold in the hut.

All I can do, he thought, is to find the old woman and make her tell me where she's hidden it.

So he set out along the path that she and her two companions had taken.

It was daylight by the time Juan reached the river. The countryside had been deserted, but here, along the riverbank, were two huts. Nearby, a man and his son were hard at work, hoeing potatoes.

It had been a long, long time since Juan had spoken to another human being. Yet his desire to find the woman was so strong that he went up to the farmers and asked, in a hoarse, raspy voice, "Have you seen a short, gray-haired woman, wearing a black cloak?"

"Oh, you must be looking for Doña Josefa," the young boy said. "Yes, we've seen her. We went to fetch her this morning, because my grandfather had another attack of—"

"Where is she now?" Juan broke in.

"She is long gone," said the father with a smile. "Some people from across the river came looking for her, because someone in their family is sick."

"How can I get across the river?" Juan asked anxiously.

"Only by boat," the boy answered. "We'll row you across later, if you'd like." Then turning back to his work, he added, "But first we must finish digging up the potatoes."

 The thief muttered, "Thanks." But he quickly grew impatient. He grabbed a hoe and began to help the pair of farmers. The sooner we finish, the sooner we'll get across the river, he thought. And the sooner I'll get to my gold!

It was dusk when they finally laid down their hoes. The soil had been turned, and the wicker baskets were brimming with potatoes.

"Now can you row me across?" Juan asked the father anxiously.

"Certainly," the man said. "But let's eat supper first."

Juan had forgotten the taste of a home-cooked meal and the pleasure that comes from sharing it with others. As he sopped up the last of the stew with a chunk of dark bread, memories of other meals came back to him from far away and long ago.

By the light of the moon, father and son guided their boat across the river.

"What a wonderful healer Doña Josefa is!" the boy told Juan. "All she had to do to make Abuelo better was give him a cup of her special tea."

"Yes, and not only that," his father added, "she brought him a gold coin."

Juan was stunned. It was one thing for Doña Josefa to go around helping people. But how could she go around handing out gold coins—*his gold coins?*

When the threesome finally reached the other side of the river, they saw a young man sitting outside his hut.

"This fellow is looking for Doña Josefa," the father said, pointing to Juan.

"Oh, she left some time ago," the young man said.

"Where to?" Juan asked tensely.

"Over to the other side of the mountain," the young man replied, pointing to the vague outline of mountains in the night sky.

"How did she get there?" Juan asked, trying to hide his impatience.

"By horse," the young man answered. "They came on horseback to get her because someone had broken his leg."

"Well, then, I need a horse, too," Juan said urgently.

"Tomorrow," the young man replied softly. "Perhaps I can take you tomorrow, maybe the next day. First I must finish harvesting the corn."

So Juan spent the next day in the fields, bathed in sweat from sunup to sundown.

Yet each ear of corn that he picked seemed to bring him closer to his treasure. And later that evening, when he helped the young man husk several ears so they could boil them for supper, the yellow kernels glittered like gold coins.

While they were eating, Juan thought about Doña Josefa. Why, he wondered, would someone who said she was the world's richest woman spend her time taking care of every sick person for miles around?

The following day, the two set off at dawn. Juan could not recall when he last had noticed the beauty of the sunrise. He felt strangely moved by the sight of the mountains, barely lit by the faint rays of the morning sun.

As they neared the foothills, the young man said, "I'm not surprised you're looking for Doña Josefa. The whole countryside needs her. I went for her because my wife had been running a high fever. In no time at all, Doña Josefa had her on the road to recovery. And what's more, my friend, she brought her a gold coin!"

Juan groaned inwardly. To think that someone could hand out gold so freely! What a strange woman Doña Josefa is, Juan thought. Not only is she willing to help one person after another, but she doesn't mind traveling all over the countryside to do it!

"Well, my friend," said the young man finally, "this is where I must leave you. But you don't have far to walk. See that house over there? It belongs to the man who broke his leg."

The young man stretched out his hand to say good-bye. Juan stared at it for a moment. It had been a long, long time since the thief had shaken hands with anyone. Slowly, he pulled out a hand from under his poncho. When his companion grasped it firmly in his own, Juan felt suddenly warmed, as if by the rays of the sun.

But after he thanked the young man, Juan ran down the road. He was still eager to catch up with Doña Josefa. When he reached the house, a woman and a child were stepping down from a wagon.

"Have you seen Doña Josefa?" Juan asked.

"We've just taken her to Don Teodosio's," the woman said. "His wife is sick, you know—"

"How do I get there?" Juan broke in. "I've got to see her."

"It's too far to walk," the woman said amiably. "If you'd like, I'll take you there tomorrow. But first I must gather my squash and beans."

So Juan spent yet another long day in the fields. Working beneath the summer sun, Juan noticed that his skin had begun to tan. And although he had to stoop down to pick the squash, he found that he could now stretch his body. His back had begun to straighten too.

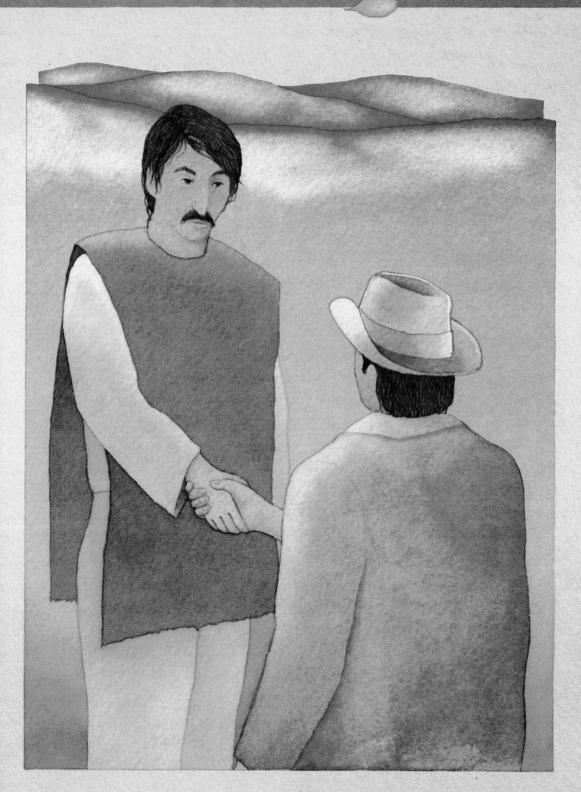

 Later, when the little girl took him by the hand to show him a family of rabbits burrowed under a fallen tree, Juan's face broke into a smile. It had been a long, long time since Juan had smiled.

Yet his thoughts kept coming back to the gold.

The following day, the wagon carrying Juan and the woman lumbered along a road lined with coffee fields.

The woman said, "I don't know what we would have done without Doña Josefa. I sent my daughter to our neighbor's house, who then brought Doña Josefa on horseback. She set my husband's leg and then showed me how to brew a special tea to lessen the pain."

Getting no reply, she went on. "And, as if that weren't enough, she brought him a gold coin. Can you imagine such a thing?"

Juan could only sigh. No doubt about it, he thought, Doña Josefa is someone special. But Juan didn't know whether to be happy that Doña Josefa had so much gold she could freely hand it out, or angry for her having already given so much of it away.

When they finally reached Don Teodosio's house, Doña Josefa was already gone. But here, too, there was work that needed to be done. . . .

Juan stayed to help with the coffee harvest. As he picked the red berries, he gazed up from time to time at the trees that grew, row upon row, along the hillsides. What a calm, peaceful place this is! he thought.

The next morning, Juan was up at daybreak. Bathed in the soft, dawn light, the mountains seemed to smile at him. When Don Teodosio offered him a lift on horseback, Juan found it difficult to have to say good-bye.

"What a good woman Doña Josefa is!" Don Teodosio said, as they rode down the hill toward the sugarcane fields. "The minute she heard about my wife being sick, she came with her special herbs. And as if that weren't enough, she brought my wife a gold coin!"

In the stifling heat, the kind that often signals the approach of a storm, Juan simply sighed and mopped his brow. The pair continued riding for several hours in silence.

 Juan then realized he was back in familiar territory, for they were now on the stretch of road he had traveled only a week ago— though how much longer it now seemed to him. He jumped off Don Teodosio's horse and broke into a run.

This time the gold would not escape him! But he had to move quickly, so he could find shelter before the storm broke.

Out of breath, Juan finally reached Doña Josefa's hut. She was standing by the door, shaking her head slowly as she surveyed the ransacked house.

"So I've caught up with you at last!" Juan shouted, startling the old woman. "Where's the gold?"

"The gold coin?" Doña Josefa said, surprised and looking at Juan intently. "Have you come for the gold coin? I've been trying hard to give it to someone who might need it," Doña Josefa said. "First to an old man who had just gotten over a bad attack. Then to a young woman who had been running a fever. Then to a man with a broken leg. And finally to Don Teodosio's wife. But none of them would take it. They all said, 'Keep it. There must be someone who needs it more.' "

Juan did not say a word.

"You must be the one who needs it," Doña Josefa said.

She took the coin out of her pocket and handed it to him. Juan stared at the coin, speechless.

 At that moment a young girl appeared, her long braid bouncing as she ran. "Hurry, Doña Josefa, please!" she said breathlessly. "My mother is all alone, and the baby is due any minute."

"Of course, dear," Doña Josefa replied. But as she glanced up at the sky, she saw nothing but black clouds. The storm was nearly upon them. Doña Josefa sighed deeply.

"But how can I leave now? Look at my house! I don't know what has happened to the roof. The storm will wash the whole place away!"

And there was a deep sadness in her voice.

Juan took in the child's frightened eyes, Doña Josefa's sad, distressed face, and the ransacked hut.

"Go ahead, Doña Josefa," he said. "Don't worry about your house. I'll see that the roof is back in shape, good as new."

The woman nodded gratefully, drew her cloak about her shoulders, and took the child by the hand. As she turned to leave, Juan held out his hand.

"Here, take this," he said, giving her the gold coin. "I'm sure the newborn will need it more than I."

Ideas Are All Around Us

by Alma Flor Ada

One of the questions my readers ask me often is, "Where do you get your ideas?" I believe ideas are all around us. Sometimes ideas make themselves very clear; sometimes one has to look very carefully to find them. Some of my ideas come from the past, from things that happened a long time ago; others have to do with things that are happening in my life right now.

One of my first original stories was about a family of dragons whose baby gets lost while pursuing a plane. These dragons were great eaters: Mr. Dragon loved trains, especially steam engines with well-lit fires; Mrs. Dragon was trying to lose weight and had limited her diet to trucks, cars, and an occasional motorcycle. . . . The idea for this story came to me suddenly on a hot afternoon while I was teaching a summer course at the University of Texas at El Paso, next to the desert. As I was walking outside returning from the cafeteria, my breath felt like fire, and since I had eaten too much, I felt like an overstuffed dragon. There was the story.

In contrast to that example of a story born in the present, from an experience of the moment, *The Song of the Teeny-Tiny Mosquito* was born from an almost forgotten experience of long ago. I grew up in Cuba, a tropical island close to the coast of Florida.

In the evenings, my parents, my sister, and I would frequently sit on the porch to share stories and to chat. Sometimes a mosquito would try to bite someone, and we would send it away with a swat of our hand. But occasionally as someone was speaking, a mosquito would fly right into the person's open mouth. Have you ever swallowed a mosquito? It isn't the greatest of feelings! A couple of years ago, memories of those evenings in Cuba came to my mind, and I thought, "I wonder what the mosquito felt when it was being swallowed?" Before I knew it, I had written this story. In it, although the teeny-tiny mosquito gets swallowed by a frog, which gets swallowed by a fish, and so on, everything ends up all right. I share this because I suspect that sometimes part of the motivation for writing is the desire to make things right.

Now I don't feel so bad about having swallowed a mosquito or two.

The Gold Coin, my story in this book, was born of a present experience. This story came to my mind already complete, as stories sometimes do. A few years ago, I was meeting with parents of the students of the Pajaro Valley School District in Salinas, California. These parents were mostly migrant farm workers. Because it was late in the spring and days were already long, the farm workers had to stay in the fields as long as there was sunlight, picking the crops. Our meeting started at almost ten o'clock and lasted until midnight.

As I was driving home through the country roads in the moonlight, I was touched by very deep feelings. I felt a great deal of admiration for the farm workers, who work very hard and get paid little, and yet endure with the hope that their children's lives will be better than their own. I thought of how valuable their work is, since it nourishes us with healthful food from the earth and therefore allows us to remain alive.

As I recalled their faces—faces tanned and wrinkled from the hours under the sun, faces filled with the dignity of honest work—I felt extremely moved and enriched from knowing them and having been able to exchange ideas with them. I felt as if, in our encounters, I had received a valuable treasure. Before I knew it, *The Gold Coin* was in my mind. I arrived home with my face bathed in tears and sat quietly through the night transferring the story to paper.

Yes, ideas abound all around us and inside us. They invite us to open our eyes and ears and bring them to life on paper.

Thinking About It

1 When did you first realize that Juan was becoming a different person? Have you ever known such a change to happen to a person? Where? When?

2 Juan's change comes in stages. That is, he changes a little at a time. What causes each change?

3 When a character changes in a story, he or she is called a dynamic character. List three dynamic characters you've read about. Tell why they are dynamic. Then create a new *dynamic* character for a story.

Another Tale of Selflessness

In *The King of the Golden River,* by John Ruskin, twelve-year-old Gluck would like to be kind and helpful to people, but his two older brothers are cruel and selfish to neighbors and to strangers. Will each of the three get his just reward?

LOVE
Until It Hurts

by Patricia Reilly Giff

In Calcutta there is a Hindu temple. It is known as Kalighat[1] It is dedicated to Kali, the goddess of death.

Kali is pictured as a statue made of black stone. Her tongue of gold hangs down over her chin, and her body is covered with gifts of jewelry from the faithful Hindus who visit her.

While Mother Teresa was still living at Mr. Gomes's house,[2] she was looking for a new place, a place to shelter the dying.

It was in a pair of rooms in the rear of Kalighat that she found it. She called it Nirmal Hriday,[3] the Place of the Immaculate Heart.

[1] Kä′li gät
[2] Between 1949 and 1953, Mother Teresa and the nuns in her order lived in a house donated to them by Michael Gomes. They then moved to a house at 54A Lower Circular Road.
[3] Nir′mäl Hrē′dā

Mother Teresa's wish to open a house for the dying began with a woman she found in front of a hospital. This woman was in miserable condition. She was caked with dirt. Rats and ants had bitten at her legs and feet.

Mother Teresa half-carried, half-dragged her inside. The people in the hospital didn't want to keep her.

Hindus believe that everything a person suffers is meant to be. That is his karma.[1] A person pays for the evil he has done in an earlier life by suffering in this life. The punishment may be sickness, poverty, or bad luck. Since there is nothing a person can do about it, he accepts it, and so does everyone else.

The hospital staff had no idea how stubborn Mother Teresa was. She told them that they had to take the woman. She'd stay until they did.

At last they took the woman in.

Mother Teresa went straight to the city hall. She needed a place, she said, a place where the dying could die, not like animals, but loved and clean and cared for.

The town officials agreed. There were those rooms, the ones in back of Kalighat. Years before, they had been used for Hindu travelers. When they came to worship Kali, they would rest in the back rooms. But now travelers didn't use the place anymore. No, now it was a hangout for drug addicts and gamblers. Mother Teresa could have it. She was overjoyed.

The place was dirty. It would probably take months to clean it up. But that was not good enough. Mother needed it immediately. She and the sisters set to work to clean it.

As soon as it was ready, a week or so later, they were out on the streets, dragging the dying out of the gutters.

[1] kär'mə

At first there were no beds in the house, but that didn't stop the sisters. They laid the dying carefully on the black marble floor.

Even though they were faced with dreadful sights and smells, they were encouraged by Mother Teresa's words: "See God in everyone you meet."

Mother Teresa and another sister help a sick child.

The sisters' faces were warm and loving as they washed the dying, as they removed maggots from their wounds, as they gave water or soup to them.

"They are Jesus," Mother Teresa said of the dying. She made sure that her sisters bent close to them as they worked, holding their hands, patting their shoulders.

Nearby neighbors began to complain. Their view of the dying was different from the Catholic view.

Why were the nuns caring for the sick? They could not change a person's karma or keep his soul from passing into a new body when he died. Did they want to make them Catholics? It was against Indian law for a person to try to change someone's religion.

The people didn't know that the dying died as they had lived. For the Catholics, there were the Last Rites of the Church. For the Muslims, sisters read from their holy book, the Koran. For the Hindus, they sprinkled precious water from the Ganges on their lips.

Some of the Hindus began to chase the sisters. They threw sticks. Then a group of men even entered the House of the Dying. They surrounded Mother Teresa and told her they were going to kill her.

She shrugged. Killing her would just send her to heaven. They backed away and left.

Then the neighbors sent a policeman to remove Mother from the temple. He stood there watching Mother clean dreadful wounds with love. He saw her care, her kindness.

He shook his head. Unless the town people would ask their own mothers and sisters to come to the temple and care for the sick, he would not make Mother Teresa leave.

The town people continued to grumble. Mother Teresa continued to carry the dying into the temple.

Mother Teresa helps the poor.

One of those people had a disease called cholera. No one would touch him. No hospital would take him. Everyone was terrified of getting cholera too.

Mother Teresa picked the man up herself. She brought him into the House of the Dying. She washed and cared for him until he died.

Then the people of the town learned that he was a Hindu. Not only was he a Hindu, but he was a Hindu priest. He had worked at the Kalighat temple before he had become ill.

Suddenly people changed their attitude toward Mother Teresa.

Neighboring women came into the House of the Dying to help. Working people came before they went to work. They'd help the sisters clean one or two of the sick, or spoon some dal—beans ground up into a broth—into a sick woman.

Doctors came, too, when they could. They helped diagnose illnesses and suggest treatment.

Help came in the way of needed supplies. Drug companies began to donate medicines. People gave old clothes, extra food. Someone sent some canvas mattresses and some small, flat pillows.

One woman, Ann Blaikie, wanted to help Mother Teresa too. She began to gather old clothes for Mother's poor. She organized her friends, and they became known as Co-Workers. Eventually people from all over the world were signing up as Co-Workers to help in Mother Teresa's work.

Mother Teresa had not forgotten the children, though. The school at Moti Jheel[1] had continued and was growing. But what about the orphans? Some of them were children of the people who had died in Kalighat. What about the children of the poor . . . children who were starving to death in front of their mothers' eyes? What about the children who were thrown out, unloved, on top of the garbage heaps?

By 1955 Shishu Bhavan[2] was opened.

Shishu was a building not far from the Mother House on

[1]Mō′tē Jēl
[2]Shē′ shü Bä′ vän

Lower Circular Road. It was unpainted, with crayoned drawings and words splashed across the walls. But Mother Teresa was glad to get it.

As soon as they had cleaned it, Mother Teresa and the sisters went out to the streets and the garbage dumps to pick up the abandoned babies and children.

Some of the babies were less than a day old. Many of them who were brought into Shishu lived for only an hour or so. They were just too small or just too sick to survive. But those who died were clean, and they had been held and loved by the sisters.

That was what Mother Teresa wanted. "Person to person," she called it. She was not a social worker out to reform the whole world. She did not want to become involved in politics. She wanted to see God in each person.

Now some of the babies were saved. Even the very little ones who were no bigger than a grown-up's hand somehow managed to survive. Mother dressed them in green-and-white-checked clothing small enough for dolls and placed them lovingly in boxes, in packing

Mother Teresa prays for the children of the world.

crates, or gently on the floor. They were cared for by smiling sisters who were as young as sixteen, as old as seventy.

Mother began to think about the children's future. They had to be raised, and, most of all, they had to find the love of a family. She began to look into the possibility of having these children adopted—in India if possible, but if not, in Europe, or even in the United States.

For those who couldn't be placed, there was still a home at Shishu Bhavan. The sisters would be their family.

But there were so many children. And so many things they needed.

Mother Teresa always worked with the closest one. She tried not to think about the others; otherwise she never would have been able to manage.

Whatever the sisters did had to be done with joy and laughter. "Go back to bed," she told one sister who seemed sad.

She wrote a memo for the blackboard in the Mother House. It said:

I prefer our sisters to make mistakes
through kindness than to perform miracles
through harshness.

And now more and more people were beginning to notice what Mother Teresa was doing. They called her mad, they said she was crazy, but they came to help anyway.

Some came with money. "I want you," she said, "not your money." She told them to give of themselves until it hurt . . . but then it wouldn't hurt anymore.

Still the people came, and so did the money.

Mother Teresa knew how to use it all. She was an Indian citizen herself now. She knew Indian culture as well as she had known Albanian[1] culture. Better perhaps.

She knew, for example, that a boy needed school. Not her Moti Jheel schooling . . . that was a slum school not recognized by the Indian government. No, if a boy was to stay out of the slum, he had to have a recognized education.

Mother Teresa became a citizen of India.

This education was not so important for a girl. A poor Indian girl stayed home to care for the younger children. What she needed was a dowry. Without it no man would marry her.

This dowry was a gift to the groom to start the new couple in their married life. Even if the dowry was only a sari, a wedding ring, a few odds and ends of furniture, it had to be found.

When people came to Mother and asked how they could help, she told them. Sponsor a child. Give a little money each month.

The girls would get their dowries. The boys would get their education.

She thought of another plan too. Suppose people sponsored a child who still lived with his poor family, perhaps the

[1]Mother Teresa's family was originally from Albania.

oldest or the brightest. If even one of a family was educated, then the rest of the family could survive with his help.

She sent the sisters to marriage brokers, people who found husbands and wives for her growing children. This was the accepted way in India. Often a bride and groom had never seen each other before the wedding.

She made sure that Hindu children were engaged to Hindus, Muslim children to Muslims, and Christians to Christians.

She even found material, sheer and lovely, for wedding gowns, and held the wedding receptions there in Shishu Bhavan, with cakes and sweets.

Shishu became a center for many activities. When Mother found boys out on the street in the late afternoon, she asked what they were doing. Learning to steal and rob, was the reply. She opened a late-afternoon high school to keep them off the streets.

She started a food line and gave rice and bananas to those who needed them. One night, when that wasn't enough, she handed the sisters' dinner plates out the door of the Mother House.

She began to think about these beggars. She had seen so many people covered with rags from head to toe, sitting in the streets asking for food. These people looked like bundles of old rags. They didn't get much help, though. They were shunned. They were told to get out of the streets. The reason? Leprosy.

Leprosy is an old disease, a feared disease. In the days of the Bible, lepers had to carry a bell and call out, "Unclean, unclean," when someone came near. In India feelings about leprosy hadn't changed. If leprosy was a person's karma, then he must have a hard lesson to learn from a past life.

People were desperately afraid of catching the disease. They feared the thickening of the skin, the loss of feeling. They were terrified of losing fingers and toes, ears, the nose.

Called by its correct name, Hansen's disease, it was less frightening. People in the West were not worried about it anymore. They knew that the disease was not as contagious as people believed. It rarely spread, except in hot climates where people were crowded together.

In the slums of India, of course, the conditions were more likely to help in the spread of the disease. And uneducated people were terrified. But there was a treatment that was especially effective if given early enough, before the disease affected nerve endings.

Lepers were afraid to say they had the disease, though. They knew they would lose their jobs and even their families. They hid the disease as long as they could—until they lost part of a finger, or until the condition showed on their faces, or until someone else in the family had leprosy too.

Mother Teresa wanted to tackle that problem next. She began to look for a place for a leper colony.

The first place she found was a spot of land between the railroad tracks. The local people found out about what she had in mind. When she went to look at the property, they threw stones. She told her sisters they'd have to go somewhere else. She had to do something. There were more than two million lepers in India, and more than thirty thousand in Calcutta alone.

Then something wonderful happened. A priest, the Reverend Alfred Schneider, head of Catholic Relief Services in Delhi, wanted to give something to Mother, a personal gift from himself.

What did she want?

She wanted an ambulance, a medical van that could go from place to place.

Schneider gave her twenty-five hundred dollars, Catholic Relief Services gave her the rest, and an American electric company sent money to be used for lepers.

Part of her problem would be solved with this ambulance. If she couldn't have the lepers in one spot, she could go to them. The ambulance could go out from Shishu Bhavan every day and treat lepers in their own communities.

Mother Teresa is recognized around the world for the work she does.

Work started in 1957. "Touch a leper," Mother told her sisters. "Touch him with love." To those lepers who had already lost a finger or a hand, to those who could no longer work at their jobs, the sisters began to teach new trades. The lepers learned how to make shoes, to weave cloth, to make bandages.

The sisters pounded away at the idea: Come early. Come when you have just one spot of leprosy and you can be cured.

Mother Teresa finally found a place for these lepers who needed to be in a sheltered community. Shanti Nagar,[1] the Place of Peace, was a place of small houses, with trees and a pond. Lepers in advanced stages of the disease could live and die among friends.

Mother Teresa was still not satisfied. There was a whole world outside, a world of sick, a world of poor, millions of sad, unhappy people.

She wanted to do more.

[1] Shän'tē Nä'gär

A Message of Love

by Patricia Reilly Giff

She is called the Saint of Calcutta, the Mother of the World. She is stooped and tiny, an old woman whose message is love. There are few people who haven't heard about her work; few people who haven't picked up a newspaper, or turned a TV knob, to see Mother Teresa's lined face squinting up at the camera. She is always cuddling an orphaned baby or giving soup to a starving child. She kneels in the street, comforting the sick and the dying.

The admiration she receives isn't important to her, though. She went to Norway in a threadbare coat in 1979 to receive the Nobel Prize. Horrified officials in India learned she wanted to work as a stewardess to pay for her flights. She certainly isn't happy that people write about her life. All that is important is her work.

To write about Mother Teresa was a wonderful experience for me. I loved thinking about her as Agnes Bojaxhiu (boy´ä jē ü), the small girl who grew up in Skopje (skō´pē ä), Yugoslavia. I wondered at her courage. How could she leave her home to become a nun and go to India at the age of eighteen, knowing she'd never return home? Years later, in 1948, how could she have left her convent to work with the poor in the streets of Calcutta? And how has she managed to help millions

Mother Teresa receives the Nobel Prize for Peace, 1979.

of people and form an order of nuns that spread across the world?

The answers are not as difficult as one might think. I found them in talking with her nuns, with her volunteers, and most of all in studying her life. It is simply that with love and determination, by helping the person nearest at that moment, we have the power to accomplish much more than we believe we can.

Mother Teresa gives her Nobel acceptance speech.

Thinking About It

1 In every age, there are people who are admired by almost everyone. As you read about Mother Teresa, what caught your attention and led to admiration?

2 Does it take a special type of person to do the kind of work that Mother Teresa does, or could anyone do it? Could you do it? Explain.

3 Mother Teresa saw a problem and acted to correct it. What problem do you see around you? What could be done to correct it?

Someone Else Who Cares

Desmond Tutu, by Patricia Lantier, is a biography of Archbishop Tutu of South Africa, a leader in the struggle against the laws that discriminated against black South Africans.

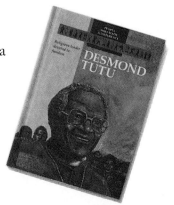

F•66

PRINCE OF THE DOUBLE AXE

by Madeleine Polland

CHAPTER ONE

Long long ago, beside the dark blue water called the Middle Sea, kings still ruled from golden thrones, and their children were princes and princesses.

The lands they ruled were hot and dry, and many of their people very, very poor. Like Lycus, a little goatherd, who rubbed his eyes and shivered one morning in the cool wind that comes before the sun. It had been a long night, and chilly, and he dare not sleep, lest a wolf from the high hills should slip with quick death through the edges of his flock. The goats drifted like small hungry shadows on the hillside and as soon as it grew light, he must number them again.

The sun came over the sea and the water changed from bitter gray to deep warm blue. Tiredly Lycus turned to the goats. He could not count, but knew still how many there should be that were black. And brown. And tawny. And white? He started and screwed up his eyes. His father had no white goat. What then had slipped quickly behind the great rock further up the hill?

His heart thumped on his thin ribs, but he reached bravely for his staff. What animal could move so quietly and cause no fear among the goats? Bigger than himself? Fear rose in his throat. He was not yet much taller than his own staff, and he could not stop his legs from trembling as he climbed the hill. At the last moment, he rushed round the rock, before his fear could stop him, clanging the heavy bell he carried to scare away the wolves.

Bell and staff together dropped to his sides, and he stood speechless. No animal crouched behind the rock, but a girl about his own age. But thin. Very thin. Her hair fell in small dark curls about her face, touched here and there with something that glittered in the sun. Her white dress fluttered in the wind, and the same bright stuff as was in her hair was all along its edges. She did not look like any girl that he had ever seen. Not like his sisters, nor any other girl. His mouth was open, speechless, trying to find words to tell her he would not hurt her, but had thought she was an animal. Before he could speak, she snapped at him.

"Put your staff down. I will not hurt you. And stop that bell."

He gaped at her. Did she not know that if he had come a little faster, her head would be crushed now as his mother crushed eggs for the cooking pot?

She was not afraid, but bright-eyed with anger.

"Put it down," she hissed again. "And sit down lest you are seen. And be quiet."

"It is my mountain," he began to say resentfully. And stopped. His father's goats, but not his mountain. Something about this girl told him she would know this and be quick to say it. Who was she?

She asked him first.

"Who are you?" she said to him, her bright dark eyes roaming his shabby person. He swaggered a little, trying to crush a feeling of being nobody.

"I am Lycus," he said. "Who are you who does not know?"

He could not hide his curiosity. Any girl should be with her mother now, grinding grain for the day's bread.

"I am the Princess Skira," she said and lifted her head on her thin neck. "I am the daughter of the king. From Knossos."

He did not understand most of it, but understood enough to make him laugh, so that the goats looked up startled from the dry grass.

Temper flushed her thin face.

"I am," she hissed at him. "I am."

"True," he said then. "And I the king himself. That is why I herd goats along the mountain." He looked at her impatiently and waited for the truth. But her mouth grew tight, and he felt suddenly uneasy.

She plucked at a fold of her dress and held it up, showing him the glittering edge. It was more like a cloud than a dress, and the sun flashed at him from the bracelets on her arms.

"Have you seen that before?" she asked him sharply. "Gold? Have you seen gold before?"

He began to sweat. Gold he had heard of, but never seen. What goatherd would see gold? He shuffled from foot to foot, his mouth dry, not knowing what to say. The goats drifted down the hill toward the sea, and he forgot to watch them.

Her face changed. She must not frighten him away.

"I am," she said urgently. "I am the daughter of the Minos. His youngest."

He could only stare. He believed her now. She pointed to the high white walls of a great house far along the hill. Lycus had been told never to go near them.

"The country palace of my uncle," she said, and could not tell him fast enough, lest fear take him away.

"I have had a fever. They sent me here to be away from Knossos in the high heat. But I wanted—"

She stopped, and he noticed suddenly that all her bones stood out like the bones of the smallest goats who could not struggle to get enough to eat.

"You wanted what?" he managed to say. He did not fear her, but his stomach lurched with the terror of some gilded spearmen bursting from the distant palace to hunt him down along the hillside, for stealing the daughter of the king!

"I have never been outside a palace," she said, and knelt up to be closer to him, the gold-edged skirts trailing in the dust. "Except in a ship. Never been outside Knossos and now here. I wanted to see." She gestured at the empty hillside. "To talk to someone not from a palace. I saw you—" she trailed off, and now looked as if she might be afraid of him. "You will not take me back?" she begged him.

Take her back? And risk a spear clean through his bones?

"What is Knossos?" was all he could say.

"My father's palace," she said in surprise. "As big as all the mountain. Did you not know?"

Before he could speak, his eyes caught a movement down the hill.

"My goats!" he yelled, and forgot the king's daughter and the royal spearmen in the real threat of his father's staff across his back. The goats were scattering themselves like small brown rocks along the smooth sand by the sea. He was off down the rough slope, nimble as a goat himself. She sat up on her heels and gazed after him.

"Skira," she called suddenly, as if it might stop him. "My name is Skira." But he couldn't hear, bounding up and down the soft sand, gathering his goats. For the moment he had forgotten her.

She glanced along the mountain toward the distant palace, then determinedly took her glittering skirts in both hands and struggled down the hill. He saw her come and could hardly count his goats, waiting for the spears to bristle on the rise behind her. But when she reached him she was weeping.

"Is it all like this?" she asked him.

"Like what?" He longed to be rid of her, but could not tell her so. Nor could he take her to his home. They would be as frightened as himself. "Like what?" he asked again.

She held out soft brown feet, bleeding from her rough stumble down the hill.

"Like this. Why do your feet not bleed?"

He looked down at his hard and horny feet, and for the first time since he had seen her, grinned.

"They do not know how to. But what did you walk on in this palace?" He could not remember the name.

"Knossos? All the courts and houses have floors

of colored tiles, smooth, and warmed underneath in the winter."

He thought of the earthen floor of his own home and sighed. Why must she talk all this nonsense while she put him in danger?

"You should go back there," he said. "Then you would not hurt your feet."

"Not at once." Her thin face was pleading. "I know I must in the end but not at once!"

He could hardly understand her. She did not even speak like him.

"Look," she said then, and her eyes were huge and sad. "Sit below in this little cliff. Then no one can see us from above. A little while. Please. Talk to me. Tell me how you live."

"How I live? Like everybody else, of course. What questions."

"Please sit," she begged him. "They could see us here."

He looked at his goats, safe on the hill again, and shrugged. But he sat down.

"What will they do if they find you with me? To me?"

Her haughty look came back, and the curled head tilted.

"They will do as I say. They will be so glad to get me back. They could even reward you."

That might be true, he thought, and his courage grew.

"Go wash your feet in the sea," he said, "to clean the wounds." She moved at once, and he felt suddenly

as if he were a little bigger. She was tiny, standing in the
edges of the sea; smaller than himself, her ankles like the
frail legs of a bird under the white skirts that billowed in
the sea wind. When she came back, the ends of her dress
were wet, and sand clotted the washed wounds on her
feet. Already she looked more like himself, and some
sudden softness made him move aside to give her a good
place to sit.

"Look," she said to him, her eyes dark and serious.
"Look. I will show you truly I am the daughter of the king.
Then you will know."

He didn't want to know. But she was pulling a ring
from her middle finger and his eyes caught the glint of gold.
Gold. He knew it now. Or was it all a dream from which he
would wake to a cold dawn on the prickly hillside, as he
had often done before?

"Don't take it off," he cried. "They will say I stole it."

But she had it in her hand.

"Look," she said urgently. "Look at it. The Double
Axe. The sacred seal of Crete. Only the family of the Minos
may wear it."

Fear filled him like a sickness, to be so close to such
a thing. These things were talked of only by the old men
who knew everything, around the crackling fires they lit to
warm their ancient bones at night. But even they spoke
only of what they had heard. Never in their long lives could
they hope to see a royal ring. Now this girl pressed it into
his hand.

"No!" he cried, and drew away from her.

"Don't be afraid. We are hidden."

There was sand in her dark hair among the threads of gold, and her eyes were excited.

He saw himself telling of this in the homestead when it was all over. He laughed suddenly and seized the ring embellished with the Double Axe of Crete, and placed it on his little finger.

"They will never believe me," he said, holding out his scarred brown hand with broken nails. She watched him, pleased to see him smile, and for a moment they were lost to everything, joined by the bond of the ring. The sun was hot on their absorbed faces, and no wind touched their small world beneath the rocks.

S houts tore them apart; distant, but fast growing nearer; a loud confused noise, and through it the bellowing of frightened cattle. They thought of nothing but the Royal Guard. Skira scrambled to her feet and did not know which way to run for shelter.

"They have come for me," she gasped, and now she was no more than a frightened child. Lycus, on his knees in the sand, felt cold terror crawl his skin, as though the spear was already at his back.

"You said . . . " he began, but got no further. Over the spit of land between them and the palace raced a herd of bellowing cattle, dark horned shapes crowded on the

brilliant sky. At the same moment, men burst down the hill behind the children, yelling and brandishing spears and staves, racing to cut off the charging animals on the open beach. Lycus and Skira stood for one hopeless moment, caught between the cattle and the men.

"Pirates," Lycus whispered hoarsely.

"What is pirates?" She grabbed his hand, her adventure in the open world turned in a moment into gasping fright. He held her tight and looked frantically for escape.

"They come to steal cattle," he said, and as he spoke, the first of the raiders were leaping the small cliff under which they had sat, scattering the goats across the hill. The empty beach was a sudden uproar of yelling men and frightened cattle, churning the pale sand.

More jumped from the cliff; the animals were held, driven toward the glittering sea.

Skira gasped.

"Look," she whispered, and Lycus nodded. His father had seen such a raid once, and warned him to take his goats and flee to the hilltop if ever he saw a strange ship along the coast. Fear of his father took over from fear of the pirates.

"The goats," he cried, and shot out of their shelter as the dark shape of the raiders' ship swept the blue sea round the point toward the beach, water flying from its banked oars in drops as bright as the gold in Skira's hair. She followed him, out onto the open beach.

One man had stayed until the last, and leaped down from the cliff as all the others were herding the cattle up the ramp of the beached ship. With a yelp of pleasure he dropped on the sand beside the boy and girl and without pausing grabbed one child in each hand. He then raced down the beach, yelling cheerfully at his friends.

It was all over before they understood that it was happening. The ramp was dragged up on screaming ropes, leaving the last few animals straying on the sand. Deep down in the ship a drum began, slow and strong, and to its steady beat the oars lifted and set the vessel fast out toward the dark blue sea.

Lycus and Skira had been pushed into a corner of the deck while the bellowing cattle were penned. He heard her give a small sharp cry. She was staring back toward the shore, no longer frightened, her pale face set with anger.

The ship was pulling swiftly from the coast under the urgent drumbeat, and the great white country palace was clear, spread along the mountain. From its rambling walls and the red tiles of its roofs, a piling mass of thick black smoke rose against the morning sky.

CHAPTER TWO

The two children were herded and bustled like the cattle to a dark opening in the middle of the lifting deck. In the dark sea-smelling passage at the bottom of some steps, they were slammed against the wall by the rushing of a huge man with jet black skin, a great whip in his hands. They heard the crack of it up above them in the sunlight and the shouts of the fighting men changed to screams of pain. Then there was silence, save for the drumbeat and the rushing sea, and their own two hearts banging with their terror.

There was no sun where they were put, hustled into a small space where the only light fell like spears between the deck planks high above their heads. The smell told them they were close beside the cattle, and a group of pale huddled faces loomed before them in the salty gloom. One of the group called out suddenly.

"It is my lady! My little lady! Oh my Lady Skira, my small love, bless the gods that you are safe!"

She fell on her knees and all the others moved excitedly, peering at Skira in the half dark and crying thanks to the gods who had saved her. She felt Lycus move uncertainly beside her, and she could hardly find her voice. She swallowed hard. It was no time to weep.

"It is the servants," she said to Lycus. "The servants from the house."

"My uncle," she cried then to them, urgently. "My father's sister. What of them?"

Lycus knew she was thinking of the burning palace. They all spoke at once, and he stared at her as she raised a small hand, and silence fell.

"Tirus," she said, and an old man with thin white hair stepped forward as best he could in the small space and bowed to her. In the shifting light, love and pleasure showed in his face.

"Lady Skira," he said sadly. "It was only dawn."

"I know," she said, and glanced at Lycus as if they shared a secret.

He could not take his eyes from her. Was this what it meant to be the daughter of a king? To have this pride and quiet calm when they had just been snatched from their land and were maybe close to death? Skira bent her head to tell the old man to continue.

"Only a few servants were up, my lady," he went on. "The first we knew was the uproar of the cattle driven to the beach. They rushed into the courts of the house, only to take any they could find and then set fire to it. We had all rushed from the house, so they took us easily. His Excellency, your uncle, I saw only as I was dragged away. He ran in his night robe to the top of the grand stairs. His short sword was in his hand. But they had by then thrown blazing torches into all the downstairs rooms. We were torn away and saw no more. My lady, I tell you, I had no chance to care for them. I saw the house . . . burning. . . . "

He could say no more.

T he sun was growing higher, and a shaft of it struck like a dusty blade to light his face, wet with tears for the people he had served all his life and could not help.

Skira moved over and touched his old face with gentle fingers.

"Do not grieve, Tirus. They will know you did all you could."

"We should have known, we should have known. We had grown easy and no longer bothered with the guards. It is so long since such a thing happened."

"From where, Tirus, old man? From where do they come?"

"From Egypt, Lady. From Egypt."

"And where are we bound for?" she asked.

He bent his head, and could not look at her as he answered; his small princess, the daughter of his king, already torn and tattered by these brigands.

"The markets in Egypt," he said sadly. "The slave markets, my lady."

"You mean we will be sold?" She could not keep the fear and shock out of her voice. That had not occurred to her. "As slaves?"

Tirus lifted his white head and looked at her.

"I must not tell you otherwise, my lady. That is what will happen."

Some of the servants began a noisy weeping, but Skira stood quite still and said no more. Although his own heart had leaped to block his throat with fear, Lycus made himself stand still, too, and show no sign of it. In a moment the girl turned away toward a corner of the hold, and they all fell back to let her go, leaving her a space to be alone. But she turned before she sat down.

"Lycus," she said, and her voice only shook a little. "Lycus, my friend. Come sit with me."

CHAPTER THREE

Night came, fading out the spears of light. A sudden wind and heaving sea tossed all of them against each other in the pitch black hold, through hours of weary sickness.

Lycus slept, worn out with fighting sickness, and when he woke as dawn glowed scarlet through the decks, the boat sped on a tranquil sea below her spreading sails.

The pirates came then and laughed at them all for their pale and sorry state, but they must keep them well to sell them. They brought great leather buckets of sea water and threw them over the prisoners and floor alike. They took out a deck plank and let the sun in above their heads, and brought them water and rough bread, and the prisoners huddled around it tired and steaming in the new sun.

All but Skira, who sat erect and quiet.

"Tirus," she said when the old man had had his food. He came stiffly and stood before her.

"Oh, sit, Tirus," she said a little impatiently. "There is no space for manners. Tirus, tell me—"

Her voice grew less certain and shook a little, and beside her Lycus knew she was as frightened as himself or any of the others. "Tirus, what will happen when we get there?"

There was silence, waiting for his answer; only the noise of the green sea rushing past outside and the snap of the great sails high above their heads. The old man spread hopeless hands.

"My lady, I do not know. I spoke once with a man taken this way. He had escaped and found his way back to Crete. I did not ask him much. How could I think it would happen to myself? And even more to you, my lady?"

His voice was sad and shocked, and Lycus looked impatient, but Skira nodded. It would be a tale from some far world that could never touch the peace and safety inside the warm white palace. But Lycus leaned over to him.

"Escape?" he cried urgently. "How, old man? How did he escape?"

Once again Tirus spread his hands and shook his head, and hopelessly they all fell silent. Through the long hot day they talked little, and Lycus fretted and fretted to try and find some plan to save them all. But in his heart the only one he wanted to save was Skira—the small princess who had made him feel a prince by calling him her friend.

The next night was better. The evening wind brought no more than a long easy swell that swept them on full-bellied sails toward their terrifying destination. In the late hot sun on the next day, they knew they had arrived.

The beat of the rowing drum began again, and all their frightened faces lifted as the sail clattered to the deck. Men shouted and oars were stilled, feet ran along the decks, and in utter, fearful silence came the last gentle bump that told them they lay against the quays of Egypt. One girl burst into loud tears of terror and with a quick, angry gesture Skira bade the nurse to keep her quiet.

"We will not," she hissed at all the others, "we will not let them see we are afraid."

Lycus saw how they all tried to obey her, but he listened to the noises of the quays outside and knew that terror lay beyond the wooden walls. It was all he could do to keep his own cold, frightened stomach steady and his voice calm as he spoke to her.

"We must keep together," he said urgently, and in the last gold glow of sunlight she looked at him sadly. He felt he had known her always; as if they had shared childhood in the same home, and not merely stumbled together on the mountain those brief days ago.

"It is up to them," she answered sadly. "Thank you, Lycus," she said then, "for all you have done for me." He didn't know how to answer. What had he done, except comfort her and help fight off his own fear? He put out a cold hand and she took it. It seemed to him the ship's hold was full of eyes, all huge with terror, all facing toward the wooden door.

**B**ut it was hot, stifling morning before it opened, and a new man swaggered in with the leader of the pirates. He was tall, his black hair groomed and smooth, and a cool look in his narrow face made Skira draw close to Lycus. This was the man who might force them apart. The boy's hand was tight around hers, and his mind ranged through all sorts of madness, like taking Skira and rushing past the two men at the door. But what would they find outside? More men, to throw them back where they had come from? Death, perhaps? It was in any case too late. The narrow door was blocked by the servants of the house being harried through it and up into the sun.

Alone in the end stood Lycus and the girl and the old man, staring at each other in the sun-shot gloom, the cries of the others dying away along the quays. Her tear-drowned eyes asked a question of the old man, and he shook his head.

"We are not safe, Lady Skira. No. I think," he said, "it will be because you are young and I am old. Not fit," he added sadly, "for a full day's work."

Skira could not answer him. The men turned back and drove them out of the door and up the steps, where they stumbled a moment, blinded by the sun. They glimpsed a golden land, stretching away beyond the bustle of the quays and the stone buildings behind them. A tawny land of dark-skinned people, drenched in blinding sun.

**T**here was little time to look at it. Nor could they see much in the town, a medley of mud-built huts and stone dwellings, touched through the heat with the dank smell of the sea. At some high-pillared gates the pirate left them, and they saw the gleam of gold between him and the stranger.

"A slave dealer," whispered Tirus, and as the pirate swaggered off, they looked after him in sad silence. Even he, who had torn them from their homes, was now something familiar to cling to.

"In," shouted the dealer, and they understood him.

Through the pillars was a vast open space. People of every color crowded it, black as night and every shade of brown, and through to strange fair ones with hair of golden silk and skin as pale as flowers. They could not stare, however amazed. The man jerked them on and stopped them in the end on the fringe of a mass of children and old men and women, all herded in small groups by men like himself.

"It is as you said, Tirus," Skira whispered, and then they all grew mute, watching people who moved among the captives, pinching here and shouting there, looking at their height and thinking how big they might grow; tossing others aside as they might toss a length of linen with a flaw.

"Like my father would bargain for new goats," thought Lycus.

Some were chosen and dragged screaming from their loved ones, as idle gold passed to the man who sold them. The hot, dusty air was full of weeping and distress and sadness, and firmly Skira turned her back. Her own black lashes were spiked with tears.

"We must not look," she said fiercely, "or we will weep ourselves."

o one bought them.

The red sun hung low in the sky and the marketplace was almost empty. Still they stood on tired legs, and their tongues were dry with thirst, old Tirus weary and patient at their sides. In their frightened minds, a new fear grew. If they were not sold, would they be killed? No man would feed a slave he couldn't sell.

Their dealer was angry, pacing up and down beside them as the cool black shadows crept across the dust. These three Cretans were hung about his neck. Too old, and too young maybe. Or perhaps from too close to home. He should have bought more ebony Ethiopians or some of these strange floss-haired creatures from beyond the Middle Seas. He tapped his whip against his sandaled foot and looked with ill temper at the few people still about the marketplace.

Like a dawn wind, a ripple ran across it, and all eyes turned toward the gates. A man stepped from a rich and splendid chair, carried by four slaves, and strode off with no glance for anyone. He wore a kilt of pleated yellow linen, ropes of gold and lapis at his neck. His sandal thongs were laced with gold as Skira's had once been. Long hair was braided into plaits around a narrow, high-boned face, and slaves ran behind him in a crowd.

The dealer snarled at his last three tired and sorry slaves, and they drew themselves up into a late, weary strength. It might be this or death.

The tall man stopped, and the narrow eyes in the tilted face ranged the almost empty market, coming to rest at last on the three from Crete. He seemed to think a moment, and none of them dared breathe. In the end he came, with long and easy strides, and as he stood and looked them over, Skira was quiet, meeting glance for glance. Lycus felt the man's eyes resting on her long and curiously. When he turned to him, he tried his hardest to look tall and strong, but could feel no more than small, helpless, and far from home. The old man stood passive; death meant less to him. But his eyes were bright, watching everything that passed.

There were some words, and even the dealer looked astonished that it was all so easily completed, as with a careless gesture the tall man bade a servant give him gold. For another long moment the tall man's eyes rested on Skira; then he turned and stalked back to his chair. A servant gestured sharply at the three to follow him, and the old man hung back. The servants gestured again, and old Tirus laid a hand upon his heart.

"Me also?" he said, not believing.

The servant nodded, this time with anger, and the man ran to follow. As they picked their way across the spaces of the empty market, and the dealer hurried off with his day's gold, they shot quick glances at each other. In the fading, dust-filled golden day, all their eyes were full of hope and wonder; they were together.

Lycus was tired and hot, and his kilt stuck to his waist. He hitched at it, easing it for coolness, and his fingers touched a small hard circle.

The Ring. The Double Axe. He had forgotten it. They had both forgotten it. He took it from the pouch and turned quickly to call Skira to give it back. It might help her prove who she was. It might even free them! Before he could speak, another servant moved over and took Skira by the arm. As he led her off, she turned, and now for the first time there was panic in her face, and she looked only what she was: a small frightened girl in a strange land, being led away into captivity.

"Skira," he yelled and would have run, but a sharp blow on his head brought him to a halt, and he was flung back to Tirus.

"Tirus," he said frantically. "Tirus." And now he wept and could not help it.

"My son," said the old man sadly. "You can do nothing. Let us only beg the gods that we may see her again."

CHAPTER FOUR

In the sudden dusk, he and Tirus were hustled onto a boat, where a wide shallow river drifted to the sea. It was long into the darkness before they moved—time enough for many indecisions and decisions as Lycus puzzled how best to keep the ring safe for Skira. In the end he slipped it on his finger, for the only other place where it might safely be carried was in the pouch of his kilt; and as all the slaves he had seen so far were dressed in the same kind of rough white linen, it seemed probable that his own kilt would be taken from him.

He lay all night in sad silence against the old man's shoulder, until dawn streaked the sky with green and scarlet as they drifted to a fine jetty guarded by tall stone animals. They seemed to the weary boy to sneer at him as though they knew his plight, but he had kept his head and marked that if the chance came to escape, they were a short night's journey from the sea.

He whispered so to Tirus as they drew in across smooth shallow water that the dawn had stained to rose. The old man nodded, but his face was gray and tired. For a quick moment Lycus wondered whether he would be alive if the time for escape ever came. The boat slid to a mooring among many others, some plain and simple. Some, close by the jetty, were painted and curtained like a dwelling.

"We go to a well-found house," the old man said, and the man in charge yelled at them to stop talking.

As Lycus turned toward the land, he saw a long log lying in the muddy shallows. Suddenly it lifted an ugly, fang-toothed head, reared a moment in the water, and then slid lazily into the river near the boat.

"Tirus," he gasped. But the beast was gone, leaving only a ripple on the glassy river. He looked dazedly with Tirus at the house. A sudden spread of green lay some distance across the dry and tawny land, a blaze of colored trees and flowers, and tall palms stirring gently in the dawn wind. Like a dream among them rose a pillared dwelling, as golden as the land itself. From it to the river ran a paved road of stone, lined by the great carved beasts, and they were taken from the boat and led along it. In amazement, Lycus gaped and stared and gaped again, but had still seen almost nothing before they were in a high-walled court. White doves circled overhead, and the morning heat was cooled by the high shadows of the palms. From inside the vast dwelling came the sounds of morning; a dog barked and some small child cried; slaves passed in a rapid stream with water jars, filling them from a stone well in the corner of the court. They stared at Lycus and the old man from the corners of their narrow eyes.

There was a cold-faced overseer in charge of all the slaves. He came to the old man and the young boy and looked them up and down, and clearly thought his master mad to buy them. In a while he went away and brought back two pale kilts the same as all the rest.

"Put them on," he said. He was heavy, great rings of fat around his waist, and his eyes deep bedded in his dark face. One hand held a short, thonged whip. As he handed the boy his kilt, his black eyes grew large and still.

"Your hand, boy," he said hoarsely. "Your hand."

In the long, frightening night, Lycus had again forgotten the ring. Now he held out both hands, puzzled, and the man stretched out a fat, frightened finger.

"The Ring of the Axe," he said and almost whispered, hushed by awe. "Is it yours? Did you steal it? No. No one could steal it. Is it yours?"

Sick fear swamped Lycus. The man's tongue was not the same as his, but close to it. Fear drove him to understand. What should he say? If he said yes, would they kill him? So if he said it was Skira's, would they kill her? How could he say it was hers, if it might lead to her death? His mouth opened and closed, and he looked wildly at the old man, but Tirus stared back at him with eyes as frightened as his own. He thought of the moment at which Skira had called him friend.

"It is mine," he said, and was shamed by his thin voice. But he had said it.

He waited, dry-tongued, for the man to snatch it or to whip out the thin knife at his waist. He barely knew what death meant. But he stood and waited for it.

Instead, the man backed off through the shadowed pillars, fear on his fat face, leaving the old man and the boy to stare at each other, trembling.

"I couldn't say it was hers," Lycus said hopelessly. "It might have caused her death."

Tirus nodded, his old face grave. He knew about death, and knew what this thin, shaking child had risked for his small princess. Before they could say more, sandals scuffed again among the pillars, and the overseer came back, struggling to keep up with the long quick strides of the man who had bought them in the market. He must have been on another boat, for he looked fresh and splendid as the morning. His black hair was sluiced with water, and drops still glittered on his brown skin.

"The ring," he said imperiously. But even his firm voice held a note of doubt and amazement. Lycus held out his hand. Why did they not kill him and be done with it? The tall man did not touch the ring but looked

at it long and close. Then he looked at Lycus, straight into his face.

"It is true, Lord Tumen," whispered the overseer, pale with awe, but the man Tumen did not turn from Lycus.

"Is it yours?" he asked him.

"It is mine," Lycus said, and now his voice was firm. Again he waited for the knife. But the man called Tumen said no more, turning back rapidly into the dwelling.

he sun was clearing the palm trees as he bowed before his mistress, who was sister to Egypt's king. She sat in a loose, pleated robe of saffron linen, flowers braided into the long black plaits of her hair. Pale gleaming gold and purple amethysts studded the ivory of her slender chair, its arms carved like claws under her thin hands.

"I hope, Tumen," she said coldly, "it is something worthwhile that makes you drag me early from my bed." Tumen bowed again, untroubled.

"Princess," he said, "it is worthwhile." He lifted his head and looked at her. "I bought two slaves yesterday. Children."

"What is that to me?" She looked bored and irritable.

"Princess. One of them wears the Ring of the Double Axe."

She stared at him as if she did not believe it. And said so.

"I do not believe it."

"Madam. It is true. I have seen it."

Still she stared, and then caught her lip in her lower teeth.

"You mean," she cried, "we have captured one of the Royal House of Crete?"

"A child, Princess, and I do not know how he was taken. Only a child. A boy. Small." He frowned a moment. "There was a girl," he said. "I would have thought . . ." He stopped. "But it is the boy who wears the ring," he said firmly.

"He stole it," she said.

"Madam. No Cretan would do so. It is cursed. Not even a child would take it."

She was quiet, knowing this true, then pleasure and mischief lit her face.

"Then he shall be mine," she cried. "A small prince of Crete shall be my toy. Find out all you can about his capture. Bring me the boy."

Tumen bowed and left, and in a while, Lycus faced the Princess Nakton for the first time. He quailed before her bright dark eyes, nor did he know where to look in the pale splendor of her room. He still thought the ring to be a thing of danger and death, so he lied quickly, and in fear, telling her he was indeed a prince of Crete.

So he hoped to save Skira.

With a cold pang of loneliness, he remembered all she had told him on the mountain about her life in the great palace. He repeated it and pretended it was about himself.

"I am a prince of Crete," he said, and did not know what to call her. "I am son to the Minos." As he said it he thought, I will soon be dead. "I think that the old man and the girl are a goatherd and his child. From the mountain near the summer palace."

He felt that should save her. They would not harm a goatherd's child. He could feel sweat running cold along his backbone in the stifling room, and waited for her to tell them to take him to his death.

"What happened?" she said. For a moment he did not understand.

"They came from the sea," he blundered then. "Pirates. They took the cattle. Fired the palace. Many of my servants were in the pirate ship."

She looked at Tumen.

"Where are they?"

"Madam, I do not know. I went late, needing only a pair of children for the fans and an old man for the garden. They do not eat so much," he added practically.

The dark, lovely lady stared at Lycus with her tilted eyes and a slow smile spread on her face. He looked back at her and looked at Tumen, and still waited for them to kill him. But she went on smiling.

"Then, Tumen," she said, and waved a fan of ivory, painted with pictures and in many colors, "then, Tumen, you must find another child for the fans. Take him." She pointed the fan at Lycus. "Take him, and dress him as befits a prince. Then bring him back."

Through airless moons of blinding heat, in the palace that stood like a green island in the sea of sterile sand, the bewildered Lycus learned slowly to be a prince of Egypt. He was kept much at his lady's side, but knew he was little more than the cat drowsing at her feet or the lean dogs that raced behind her chariot. Another pet. A toy.

But she gave him friends and teachers to be with him always, and they did not understand him. How could a prince, even of a small country, be unable to throw a spear; or draw a flower; or press into wax the symbols of his own speech? He could not hold a horse behind his gold-painted chariot nor catch the wind in the square sail of a boat on the wide yellow river.

He knew nothing of their strange gods—men with heads like animals. He learned with horror that the moving logs in the river were great beasts called crocodiles, who could devour a man with one crash of terrible teeth. He knew none of it. They were jealous and would be glad to do anything to harm him, so they told the Princess Nakton all of this. He was not a prince, they said. Could not be a prince.

She shrugged her narrow shoulders and waved them away.

"What do we know of his country?" she said, and would not listen. "He may do many things that we know nothing of."

In the hot silence when Lycus was alone, he stared at the ring on his finger and marveled it should do so much. Now he did not know how to stop it all. All he did know was that it had lost him Skira, when he had tried to save her.

She was in the palace, even though they had not seen her on the journey from the sea. They had got another girl to pair with her, and through every blazing day, he had to watch her, waving a heavy fan of curling colored feathers, to keep the hot air moving around in the princess's chair. While she did it, weariness plain on her thin small face, he must sit where she could see him, in his ivory chair, eating from fine painted plates, or picking at a lute that his goatherd's fingers touched with astonished skill. His guilty and unhappy eyes watched the sweat on her face and saw her dark eyes glaze with exhaustion.

She would never look at him. Her glance, in which he felt her hate, passed through him to the painted wall. Nor could he ever hope to speak to her. Sadly he knew that he was living now as she had lived, with the smooth marble floors and painted walls. Slaves ran to do his smallest bidding. This was what she had talked of on the mountain.

He couldn't tell her what he was doing. Couldn't tell her anything to take the frozen look of betrayal from her face. Couldn't tell her that in the first place he thought the ring might be her death. Now there was no going back, but there was a growing hope that as a prince, he might find some way to help them all. To get them all away. But what? He twisted the hated ring on his finger, bound to slavery as close as Skira's own, living with her bitter face that told him clearly he had stolen it. He had chosen to be a prince while she waved the heavy fan above his royal head.

hrough the stifling nights he tossed on his carved couch, and heard the night birds sing among the flowers, and could think of nothing he might do. He had learned to count the time as the palace people did, and remembered afterwards that it was in the Time of the Oryx that his plan began to creep with sick excitement round the edges of his mind.

First he grew proud and rude about the palace, where he had been the quietest and most humble of princes. He learned to clap his hands and shout at slaves and threaten to throw them to the crocodiles. Then he began to argue with his tutors. He demanded this and that, and fell into high, haughty rages if he had to wait for anything.

His surprised teachers went to the Princess, who yawned behind her fan.

"He grows," was all she said. "And he has been lonely for his own people. Now he begins to be himself. Did you think a prince could remain forever meek and silent?"

She was pleased and kept him more than ever with her. With a sick heart he watched hate harden even more in Skira's eyes, but he was careful to treat her like the rest.

He took to having whims to do strange things; he pretended not to know just what he wanted to learn. Frequently he walked his tutors through all the gardens; but the Sun God had driven many times across the brazen sky before he finally found Tirus. The old man crouched in cool-smelling shade beside a pool, where dark palms arched across the sun. He was fishing among the roots of floating flowers.

"These," cried Lycus, imperiously. "I would know of these flowers that grow in water." His heart tore him to see the thinness of the old man's body and the fear that sprang at once into his face. Fiercely Lycus waved away his servants and companions.

"I have told you," he shouted at them, "and so has my Royal Mistress. I will learn these things for myself. Can this old one harm me? Get back and leave me speak. Come, old man, and tell me of your flowers."

He was cold and hollow with excitement and fear. What more secret place to talk than crouched beside Tirus at the edge of the dank, smelling tank? How could they know what they spoke of? He could feel the old man shaking with terror at his side, and saw the glances he threw over his shoulder at the watching men.

"Tirus, Tirus." Lycus plunged his hands into the green water and gazed firmly at the flowers, as close as he dare go to the old man. "Tirus. Listen."

Tirus shook and the water trembled with his fear.

"They will throw me to the crocodiles," he said hoarsely.

"They will not," Lycus said. "I will have them thrown instead. Remember, they think I am a prince of Crete."

Tirus slid him a glance of sadness and reproach.

"Tirus, you must speak to her. Can you speak to her? Tell her why, Tirus. You know I did it first because I thought they might kill her. I cannot ever speak to her. You must tell her that. You know it's true!"

He heaved a pile of dripping roots out of the water.

"For pity's sake, finger these with me as though you tell me what to do. You know I did it for her sake."

"It is true. I know."

"But she doesn't, and she hates me. I see it in her face."

Wildly he pulled and teased at the roots and plunged them again in the water as if the old man had told him what to do. Green slime stained his colored kilt, and clung about his fingers. "You must speak with her. Tell her first why I did it. And then tell her—no, tell her nothing."

He gasped a little, and even he looked over his shoulder at his servants.

"I will come again. And again. You will do everything I tell you, and tell her what I say."

Tirus rose to his knees, and there was no hope in his face, only despair and fear. Lycus cut him short, leaping up from beside him.

"That is enough, old man," he cried. "I am bored. I will come again and see if my water flowers have grown." He turned with haughty face to his tutor. "Come," he said. "Bring me fresh clothes and then I am in a mood to paint these flowers I have seen. Then we will sail upon the river."

He lifted an idle hand toward Tirus.

"Care for him," he said. "I will speak to him again." They shrugged and lifted their fine eyebrows, but the terrified old man was left in peace.

CHAPTER FIVE

From then on they watched him, and did not know what to say. There seemed no end to his new sudden interests.

"Tell me about the river," he said one day to his tutor. Every day the wide, sluggish water grew lower in the heat, and crept almost motionless between its sandy banks. No breeze stirred sails, and boats were driven only by the sweat of half-starved slaves along the oars. In the drying mud the scaly crocodiles lay still, as if even they were too tired to follow the shrinking water.

"What happens?" Lycus asked, and his mouth was dry with his growing fear. The only way he knew to freedom was along the river. "What happens when it dries up completely?"

They dared not laugh, but smiled behind their thin, ringed hands. "This does not happen. Some moons ago, rain will have fallen in the great mountains where the river is small. It takes the water many moons to come as far as here. But soon, soon the river will begin to rise again, and spread over the land, giving fertile soil for all the crops."

"And the river grows deep and fast?" he asked.

"Deep and fast, my lord. And grows faster, so for a while a man may make the sea without sail or oar."

He wanted to leap up and down, filled with sudden hope—to race through the palace to find Skira and tell her of this thing. But he kept his face blank.

"When does it happen?" he asked, and tried to look as if he didn't care.

They told him, and Lycus counted on his fingers at his back. He still knew wonder that he could count and give the numbers names. His strange life had taught him this.

Carefully he nodded, and knew that he had a lot to do and not much time to do it. He kept on pretending to care for flowers, especially the pale pink fragile ones that Tirus grew upon the water. He often asked to paint them, saying they were the loveliest in the garden. The Princess smiled at him, and told him how pleased she was to find him loving beauty, and Lycus dropped his lids and could not meet her eyes. His skin crawled with terror lest they find what he was up to and drag him screaming to the scaly beasts along the shallows.

One thing kept him going. In quick, snatched talk above the wet stems of the flowers, Tirus told him he had talked with Skira.

"I am old," he said and shrugged. "They do not notice me much, and know my lady and I are both from

Crete." He shrugged again. "And if they kill me, what of it? I am old enough to die."

Lycus glared at him and forgot the flowers.

"No talk like that, old Tirus. I promise you will see Crete again."

The old man smiled and did not answer, as if he took it for child's talk, and the crocodiles and quick death were all he really hoped for.

"You told her?" Lycus hissed.

"I told her."

"Well, keep seeing her. Get them used to seeing you together. They will not harm you because of me." He grinned, trying to bring a smile to the tired old face.

"I make a good gardener, Tirus?" he asked.

Now the old man smiled.

"You work hard, little goatherd," he said. "May the gods grant you harvest."

The gods had granted him something already. The glare of hate had gone from Skira's eyes. Now she watched him carefully, as if waiting for a signal. He in turn watched the sinking river, and did not know when he could give it. The brazen, stifling days crept on, when the last breath of breeze died across the sun-baked mud, and even the feather fans failed to stir the airless rooms.

Lycus began to walk about at night. He padded the cool floors and remembered what Skira had told him of her palace. When he first began to do it, his servants leaped also from their sleeping mats and padded after him around the sweltering, silent rooms. He turned and snarled at them like a spoiled, ill-tempered princeling, and they fell away, whispering among themselves. They did not

know what to do. Before they could tell the Princess, he went to her himself.

"Madam," he said, and tried to look small and sick with weariness, "I am close to dying of the heat. It is much hotter than my own country, and I miss the sea. I do not sleep and like to walk the palace in the nights when it is cool and empty. Madam, I beg these servants leave me alone. I do not need them, and they follow me like my dogs."

He could hear himself, spoiled and irritable, and thought sadly how his father would settle all his grumblings with a quick thump on the ear. But the Princess looked at him with concern. He grew thinner in the heat, and fevers of all kinds ran through the palace in these last days of the dying river. She was afraid for him and would give him anything he wanted.

"Leave him alone," she told his servants. "If he wants to walk alone at nights, then let him do it."

Gladly they left him alone and stayed stretched on their rush mats, sleeping deeply in the heat they knew.

All the palace guards and servants grew used to Lycus pacing through the dead hours of the night, and as they stopped watching him, he went a little further and a little further and a little further. In the end, he could walk unheeded to the far end of the jetty, where the stones still held the baking heat of day. Below him in the mud, a crocodile would stir and move a little, and then grow still, like a log in the pale light of the waxing moon.

He looked at the boats that could barely moor at the jetty. He must have one big enough to reach the sea. Not too big, for how could three of them handle it? Three of them? The old man grew fragile as the sticks that held his plants, and Skira had the starved face of a slave. Even he, who spent all the time he could on the water, could not do everything for three of them. He felt young and useless and full of doubts, but he could think of nothing else.

The moon grew to the full, and when the arid desert was flooded with pale light, he took a boat. The guards did not care. They had all been told to let him do whatever he wished, and through all the nights of the high moon he rowed the sinking water. Even when his tutors were told, they did not bother to tell the Princess. Heat lapped the palace like a dream that stole away men's minds.

The Princess told him one day of all that was to come.

"You shall see, small stranger," she said, "when the river floods, how Egypt holds a festival."

She was looking at him strangely, and he felt suddenly cold. Her eyes were narrow, watching him. What did she know? Or think? He answered her as quietly as he could.

"We have festivals in our own country, Madam."

"What do you sacrifice?"

"Sacrifice?" He was a poor boy, and a jug of milk poured out for the gods could ill be spared. Sometimes a pigeon, if the arrows had been true. His tongue felt thick. He was supposed to be a prince, and a prince would know what was done in the House of the King. From far away he remembered tales.

"A bull," he said hoarsely. "The young people dance with the bull and then it is killed for the god."

He hoped that was right. She would know. Her black eyes were still sharp on his face.

"So I have heard," she said, and he breathed a little more. But she went on, "A mere animal would not do for the gods of our river, who send water for all our crops. They want more than an animal."

He stared at her, and understood, his tongue dry as the mud on the river.

"The crocodiles?" he asked her.

"The crocodiles."

"They are given people?"

"What else?"

"Any people?" He did not know how to put it. She shrugged.

"Slaves. But always young." She paused. "And always girls."

From the corner of his eye he saw Skira shrink. The Princess turned languidly and looked at the two girls with the fans.

He could not wait to get down on his knees beside Tirus, who sieved fresh earth carefully into the pool.

"Why do you do that, old man?" he demanded loudly for the benefit of his companions. Bored, they turned away and talked among themselves.

"Tirus," he whispered urgently. "I had a plan. It must be changed. Skira is in danger."

He told him, and the old man's face grew sad and gray. What could a small goatherd do to save his young princess?

"You must tell them," he said fiercely. "Give up the ring."

"And go myself to the crocodiles? She would not want that. Nor would they believe me."

For a moment he knew doubt. He did not have much to do with Tumen, who was concerned only with the household of the Princess. But when occasionally he met him, Tumen's eyes would rest on him even now with quiet thought that troubled Lycus. Tumen might believe.

He could not risk it. He leaped up suddenly as if struck by an idea.

"I like this ancient," he said, and waved a hand at Tirus. "Clean him up. I will have him as my body-slave. He shall sleep across my door."

They looked tired and bored. They had had too much foolishness from this stranger prince. One of them moved over and gave a sharp order to the old man. Tirus looked for one amazed second at Lycus and then did what he was told.

"Shall we tell the Princess?" one tutor asked another as the bent old figure shuffled off.

The other snorted.

"We tell her much. She only laughs and says he is a stranger. She lets him do as he likes. So we shall."

For the next three nights Lycus marched proudly through the dark palace and down to the boats, followed by his new body-slave. He watched the moon anxiously, coming to the full, and he could hear storms rumble far up the river. No guard raised his head. The strange prince was touched with madness. What matter if he killed himself or fell to the snapping jaws in the muddy water? No concern of theirs. They drowsed over their spears and did not even watch.

Out on the low and sluggish yellow river, with no light but the sinking moon, Lycus talked urgently with Tirus.

The old man shook his head.

"I am too old," he said. "Too old." He nearly wept. "I cannot do it. I am too old for slavery and it has almost killed me. I am too old. Tell them, goatherd, who you are. Tell them. It is the only way."

Lycus grew angry.

"You are old, old man," he cried, "and do not mind to die. I am young and have my home in Crete. And I will take Skira back where she belongs. It would have been easier to wait for the flood, but I dare not. If you will not come then I will take her alone. And they will throw you to the crocodiles," he added fiercely, "because you have helped me!"

In the pale light, the old man looked at him.

"You are fierce, little goatherd," he said.

"I have been a prince for many moons," said Lycus shortly. "Will you help me?"

Tirus looked the length of the long boat and sighed.

"You could not do it alone," he said. "You need me. I will come."

On the next night Lycus stopped beside the guard at the pillared gate. He snapped his fingers at Tirus.

"Last night," he said, "I was hot out on the water. Bring me the slave of the fan."

Tirus did not ask which one. He bowed and vanished like a shadow. His head in the air, seeing nothing, under the bored eyes of the guards, Lycus swept down the long jetty to his boat. Behind him marched his body-slave and his young slave of the fan.

There was no time for talking.

"Tonight?" Skira gasped as they climbed down the steps into the boat. The river could barely float it.

Lycus shook his head, and had to hold back all the things he could say to her.

"Let them see us come back," he said. "Some guard might have wit enough to see I am with two of my own people."

She looked disappointed and angry, and Tirus spoke into the night.

"My lady, he is right. It has taken him a long time to do this."

Skira was silent a moment, then she smiled.

"Then I had better do what I came for," she said, and set the great fan of scarlet feathers waving above their heads in the stifling night.

Two nights more they walked one behind the other down the long jetty between the stone animals, and each night they came back. On the third night, with nothing said, Tirus and Lycus lifted the heavy oars and started off with desperate, silent purpose down the middle of the river.

"How long?" Skira asked. Her teeth chattered with her fear. "How long until they miss us?"

Lycus shrugged.

"Morning," he said. "You are with me. There are many in the palace who will not search for me too hard, unless the Princess be at their backs with whips. Come, Skira, you must watch. The river is dangerously low, and if we go too far to either side, we are aground. Take the steering oar and keep us straight. I wish we could have waited for the flood. They tell me it brings wind."

It took all his spare breath to say that, and they did not speak much more save for warning cries from Skira now and then. Lycus was young, and Tirus old, and the flat boat heavy and unwieldy. The moon set in the end, and clear white starlight drenched the river, but they could not tell how far their fear-driven oars had taken them, nor how long they had been on the water.

Skira began in the end to weep, crying hopelessly that she could see nothing, and when in the end the boat scrunched against the drying mud, Lycus could do no more than lay his head down on his crippled arms.

"Oh," she cried, "it is all my fault. But I can't see!"

Lycus lifted his head.

"Do not blame yourself. We are too tired to keep it straight."

The old man said nothing, crumpled over his oars.

"But, Lycus," Skira whispered, and now her fear was too great for tears, "what shall we do? How far are we away? They will come and get us! Can we push it off?"

Lycus forced his stiff body to get up. They seemed to have been rowing since the gods were young, but there was no way to know. The stars were paling, but no streaks of dawn showed yet in the sky. Darkness was complete. He felt his way to the side of the boat, and Skira stumbled to join him. He looked down into the dark water.

"We have disturbed them," he said.

"What?" Her voice was a breath of fear.

Something bumped against the side of the boat, and they could just see the ripple in the muddy water.

"Crocodiles," she said.

"Yes." Lycus was almost too tired to care and the old man had not lifted his head. "Yes. We are stuck fast and cannot go on. Nor can we get out to push."

CHAPTER SIX

They were held there in black night with neither moon nor stars, and the heat lay damp on their skins although they were cold with fear. The old man never raised his head, and in panic Skira pulled at him to tell them what to do. He did not move, and in the end Lycus took her hands and held them.

"Leave him," he said. "Leave him." He felt wise and sad and very calm now that he knew there was nothing more to do. "Leave him. He is better not to know." Secretly he thought the old man dead and was afraid to go near him himself.

She grew quiet then and crept up together with him underneath the steering oar, watching the dark sky and saying nothing, waiting for dawn and the high prows of swift boats that would be searching for them.

Lycus stirred after some time and reached for Skira's hand. She felt the warm gold of the Ring of the Axe slipping over her finger.

"Here," he said. "When they come, I will tell them who you are. They will blame me for pretending to be you."

He felt her crying in the darkness and did not know what more to say. It had all been his fault. Maybe they would not kill a real princess? He dared not let himself think of the crawling monsters of the river.

They heard sounds at times, soft splashes and once the cries of men, somewhere in the far distance. Lycus searched for the lights of boats, but there was nothing. Only the thick dark, and silence, and nothing to do but endless waiting. They did not know how long they had sat there when the boat first moved. Lycus felt he had grown into an old man like Tirus, but it was still night. So at first they did not know what happened. They thought a crocodile had heaved against them in the shallow water, and clung together lest it tip the boat. Then the craft moved again, softly, gently, and swung a little from where the bows were held fast in the mud. Still they did not understand. Storm rumbled in the black sky and their clinging hands were damp with terror, for at this fearful moment, what could be happening that would not end in death? It was Lycus who first started to his feet, suddenly recalling the bored voices of his teachers when he asked them of the rising river.

"Skira," he gasped, and stumbled away from her. "Skira, the oars!" The boat had lifted from the mud and was drifting slowly but firmly to the middle of the river. All around them, he sensed the water moving gently and thought again of what they had said. It would take you without oars or sail right down to the sea.

"Skira," he screamed again, and she came with him, stumbling in the pitch dark in the rocking boat. "Skira, get the oars."

They would need them if they reached the sea! The sea!

He was shaking, forgetting his fear of the old man as he pushed past him to grab his oars. He was too late. As he reached for them, they splashed into the water. Madly he scrambled for the others, only to watch them go, pulled out by the turning boat. There was only the one still held by the old man. Frantically Lycus hung across the side. The boat swung gently underneath him and he could see the oars pale in the darkness. He dared not go in.

Skira was at his side, her teeth chattering.

"What, what shall we do now? What shall we do?"

"The steering oar!" Lycus shouted. "Keep it straight."

"What is straight?" screeched Skira helplessly. The boat had circled in the eddying river, and they no longer knew which way they faced. But they scrambled and stumbled to the steering oar, suddenly heavy and alive with water moving against it. In the dead, shallow river, even Skira had held it steady without help. Now they had to both hang on it, and in the end they managed to pull the boat from its circling.

"Keep it with the water!" Lycus cried. "With the water!" The river did not seem to be rising fast, and it would steady as it grew deeper. He thanked all the gods in one frantic second for his time as a prince. It had taught him all about the river.

"Look," cried Skira, with what small breath she had. "Look."

The banks were distant. The river here had been no more than a sea of mud. Now lights were springing all along its edges. Torches flared and spat and flamed to life, and great fires leaped into the sky. Faint across the flat spaces they could hear the shouts and cries of the people, storming to the shore.

"It will be festival now," said Lycus in a whisper and thought again of the crocodiles.

Soon, the sky began to pale, but they had no breath to speak of it. In silence they watched the first streaks of scarlet rise above the yellow land, and when the great chariot of the sun drove into the sky, Skira almost dropped the oar.

"Hold on," yelled Lycus. "Hold on."

They looked about them, and fear came cold again.

"We are nowhere," said Skira. "Are we in the sea?"

"No." Lycus looked down at the water, his arms tight with pain from the weight of the oar. The river moved under them, sleek and quiet, but flowing fast and steady for the sea. All about them was water. Water, spreading to the land in the far distance, no more now than a streak of yellow with the black smoke of the festival fires rising in the windless day. Here and there, islands of sand and mud still stood up from the water, and Lycus murmured again to the gods, begging for strength to turn the boat if they should be swept toward one.

The sun drove higher, and heat and thirst began, and still they rode helpless for the sea. The islands of sand grew fewer, and the smoke columns faded to dark smudges where the water met the far dark stripe of land.

"We must be in the sea," whispered Skira, and did not know if it would be good or bad.

"Not yet," said Lycus, and knew it would be bad. Skira had long since tired, and although she held bravely to the oar, her hands made no difference. Lycus alone held the boat with the run of the river, and knew that he, too, was almost at the end of what he could do. He could never hold It when they hit the open sea. The old man had slipped sideways, and lay against the ribs of the boat. Lycus could not go and look, but his sad mind told him surely he was dead.

They hit the sea in the high heat of the sun, and Lycus did his best. On the voyage down, he had noticed that the sun rose always on his holding hand. To go back then toward their own land, he must keep the first sight of the sun god to his working hand, and watch him through the day across his head. He had not dared think of night.

But the first cross waves of the open sea pulled the

steering oar from his torn hands, and he could do nothing. They were helpless. Dark, dark blue sea, and in the curling edges of the waves the strange blue-green of the jewels he had worn in his brief time as a prince. Lapis, they called them. He felt strange. It was easier to think of foolish things like jewels than try to keep the boat against the sea. His lips were already cracking in the hot sun, and he was dazed and stupid.

Skira stood over him, frightened. She too knew that the old man was dead, and now Lycus looked ready to follow him.

"You are tired, Lycus. You did too much with the oar." He barely saw her. She shook him as he sank to the deck.

"Do not go to sleep!" she shouted at him, angry in her fear for him. "In this sun you will die."

He shook himself, and saw her mouth as dry and painful as his own. She lurched above him in the drifting boat, and glared at him.

"Do you want to die, like Tirus?"

He did not think she had noticed.

"Look!" She pushed him sharply to keep him awake. "I have found a canopy. We can sit under it, until the sun goes down."

"If we are here," thought Lycus and struggled to his feet.

They had not the strength to raise the canopy, and they crouched under it in the high heat of the sun,

F•127

sheltering below embroidered birds and flowers, with golden tassels dangling round their faces.

They were hours silent, with no sound but the lap and splashing of the sea, and the creaking of the boat against its pressure. The change from high sun to the first cool violet dusk had almost gone unnoticed, and for a long time they did not lift their heads, although both of them could hear the shouts that came suddenly across the water. They came like voices in a dream that they need not heed. Skira moved first in the end, as slow as sleep, and pushed aside the golden tassels.

"Lycus." Her throat was tired with thirst. She croaked. "Lycus, it is a ship."

"A ship?" He did not seem to know the word.

"They are shouting at us. To get out of their way, I think."

With great effort he lifted the canopy. The side of a ship reared like a wooden cliff over their tired heads, dark against the sky, round heads lined against the blue evening.

"A pair of children," yelled a voice as if someone had asked a question. "An old man. Maybe dead."

They could see the thin bearded faces of the rowers through the holes in the ship's side; hear the rattle of their chains as the oars were drawn in. Tears sprang to Skira's eyes, as though she got the very smell of slavery.

"They will take us," she cried. "It will all be the same again."

"Throw them a rope," called another voice. As the rope snaked down to their tossing craft, the oars were beginning to creep out again. They must be quick or they would be left. Lycus grabbed the dangling rope. It would not be thrown again.

"We must go," he urged her. "That or death."

She looked a second at the starved body of the old man, and reached out and touched his head.

"Go in peace, old one," she said, "over the dark river."

Then she grabbed the rope. She and Lycus were small and light, and, scrabbling with their feet, they managed to scramble up the wooden cliff, between the oars. Strong arms heaved them in the end over the shield wall.

They stood then as they had stood before, in the middle of a ring of men, and now hope choked them as fear had done the last time. They trembled and waited. The men seemed less hostile. And had they not dragged them from the sea?

"Who are you," asked one of them grinning, "who go to sea with no oars and a dead ancient?"

Lycus began to explain, but Skira laid a hand on his arm, and then stepped forward. She held the ring up where all of them could see.

"I am a princess of Crete," she cried, "torn from my home by pirates. This is my friend. We have been enslaved in Egypt. Take us, I beg you, to my father!"

There was a long moment and the shadows seemed to grow more dark. Lycus waited sickly for them to laugh and then toss both of them back into the sea. Instead there was a silence and no sound save the hollow drum and the long swish of the sea. A man, tall and strong, and his hair the color of wheat at harvest, sprang suddenly from a sort of platform in the middle of the deck.

"Show me," he commanded, and once more she held up her hand, standing herself now in powerful silence. Like Tumen, the ship's master did not touch it, but moved back a step or two.

"Truth?" he asked her.

"Truth," she cried, and seemed with every moment to grow a little taller. "By all the gods of Minos it is truth. By the sacred bulls and the dark snakes of Ariadne, it is truth! Who could steal it?"

There was respect on the master's fair face and a little fear. He believed her.

"Your royal father," he said then, "has offered gold through all the Middle Seas for news of you. We sail for Greece. There will be Cretan ships at mooring, and we can hand you over."

Skira nodded, satisfied, and seemed to know what he was speaking about, but Lycus fell silent and would not share her pleasure, defending himself against a world he did not know. He drifted away from her while they sought food for them, and a warm soft rug to wrap the girl against the evening chill. Between the shields, he looked out at the darkening sea. In the purple distance was a small speck, lifting to the waves, and he knew it for the boat with old Tirus dead in it.

It was all that was left of his world as a prince.

He stayed so long that Skira came to get him, as if she were still his slave, sharing the food and showing him where they were to sleep, warm and sheltered on the high poop. He felt cold and sullen. He had set out to save her, so that she might be a princess again, and now that he had succeeded, he was lost and lonely, not knowing his own place.

"Why did they save us?" he asked abruptly. "They did not know who you were."

She shrugged in the near dark, and shot a glance at him.

"They are people of the sea," she said. "Like us. They care for each other on the water. They would rescue anyone."

"Like us?" Lycus was bitter and could not hide it. As a goatherd he had not known he belonged to people of the sea. Skira went on evenly.

"I know of Greece. In the time of my father's father they paid us tribute. Now they come to trade. I have seen the ships moored below my father's palace."

He was silent and did not want to know. In a while, her blistered hand crept into his, and he could hear the mischief in her voice.

"Lycus," she said softly. "I do not know about goats!"

Still he could not laugh, but they talked no more, slipping into the dead sleep that came of knowing they were safe; sleeping right into the red hour of dawn, when the drum woke them as they slid into a busy harbor at the foot of a vast cliff, towering to the milky sky. Far on the summit, buildings spread themselves as if carved from the cliff itself, touched to gleaming white by the first sun of morning. The harbor below still lay shadowed by the night.

Shadows were gone, and the moorings were steeped with hot light by the time they tied up at the stone quays. The men hung back now from Skira and looked at her with fear. Only the master spoke, saying respectfully that they should take her first of all to the King of Athens.

"You will do no such thing," she cried and stamped a royal foot, still caked with the mud of Egypt and stained with the green slime from the bottom of the boat. "You will take me at once to a Cretan ship, and if you do not then it will go ill for you when I reach my father."

Lycus thought with wonder of the times he had behaved like that, and grown men had leaped to do his bidding. For him, all that was at an end. Sadly he watched the master striding along the quays to the mooring of a high-prowed craft. It was painted and gilded like the palace in the sand, and its narrow prow ended in a golden dolphin crowned with flowers.

What was there for him now?

How could he be a goatherd again, when he had once been a prince?

There was shouting from shore to ship, and small men in colored kilts leaped at once onto the quay, staring and talking with excitement. Skira lifted her dirty face and pushed back her tangled hair, and began to walk firmly toward them. Lycus hung back.

"What of me?" he said. "What of me? No one will pay a reward for me."

She stopped and turned to him slowly, and there was something in her face that shamed him. She lifted her hand to show the ring.

"When you wore it," she said, "you used it to care for me. Shall I not use it now to care for you? Come. Let us go to my father."

She took his hand and led him along the sunlit quay. Both of them looked as old and tired as Tirus himself, and as though they walked back from some dreadful dream. But the men from the Cretan ship were grouped now to make a welcome; smiling; waiting for the slow coming of their weary princess and her friend. From the prow below the dolphin, a banner broke into the wind, dark, dark blue as the Cretan seas, with the Double Axe embroidered on it in bright gold.

Pulling the Theme Together
L E A D E R S H I P

1 Suppose that *Prince of the Double Axe* became a movie. What two scenes might people talk about for weeks after they saw the movie?

2 "I got lost in a good novel," says someone. If that someone is you, what do you mean? What in a novel can make you get lost in it?

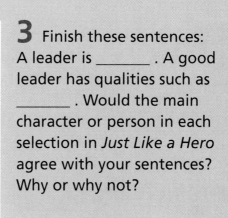

3 Finish these sentences: A leader is _____ . A good leader has qualities such as _____ . Would the main character or person in each selection in *Just Like a Hero* agree with your sentences? Why or why not?

BOOKS TO ENJOY

Sequoyah's Gift
by Janet Klausner
HarperCollins, 1993
In the 19th century, Cherokee leader Sequoyah watched as Native Americans were moved from their homelands. He dedicated himself to creating a system of writing the Cherokee language to maintain the tie his people had to their heritage and each other.

Racso and the Rats of NIMH
by Jane Leslie Conly
Harper, 1986
Will Racso fulfill his dream of becoming a hero? Why is he so insistent on helping the rats in Thorn Valley?

The Trouble on Janus
by Alfred Slote
Harper, 1986
Jack Jameson and his robot buddy Danny uncover deception and tyranny on the planet Janus.

Harriet Tubman: Conductor on the Underground Railroad
by Ann Petry
Crowell, 1955
When Harriet Tubman discovered she was going to be sold, she made a daring escape. But her heroism didn't stop there. She returned again and again to lead hundreds of slaves to freedom.

The Bread Winner
by Arvella Whitmore
Houghton Mifflin, 1990
If a grown man can't support his family, how can his twelve-year-old daughter? Sarah has a plan to save the family from the misery and poverty of the Depression.

All Times, All Peoples: A World History of Slavery
by Milton Meltzer
Harper, 1980
Slavery has a history as old as humanity. Meltzer describes how from the beginning of time people have bought, owned, and sold other people.

Characterization   An author can tell a reader directly what a character is like or can use the character's actions and speech to reveal the person's nature. A character who changes, usually as a result of what happens during the story, is called a dynamic character. At the beginning of "The Gold Coin," Juan wants to steal Doña Josefa's gold. At the end, he has changed and gives the gold coin to someone else. The change in his character is shown through his words and actions.

Foreshadowing   Hints or clues about what will happen later in a story are called foreshadowing. When Lycus first sees Skira, he thinks she looks different from any girl he has ever seen. His observation foreshadows his discovery that she is a princess. Lycus's fear of the royal ring hints that the ring will cause some problem in the future.

Narrative Poetry   A narrative poem tells a story. "Barbara Frietchie" tells a simple story of bravery—the courage of a ninety-year-old woman standing up against an army. The poetic choice of words and the rhythm and rhyme make it a narrative poem rather than a piece of prose.

Novel A novel is a self-contained piece of fiction that is longer than a short story. All novels include the story elements of setting, characterization, plot, and theme. For example, in the historical fiction novel *Prince of the Double Axe,* the theme "no matter how much trouble you face, using your wits will always help you take charge" holds the story together. The settings of ancient Crete and Egypt are integral, or necessary. The characters, too, are important to the plot. Because they are brave, they escape and bring the plot to a satisfactory close.

Plot The plot is the series of events that make up a story. Often the plot moves forward because of a conflict between characters or because a character has a problem to solve. In "Emergency!" Jeffrey, while baby-sitting, has to decide what to do when Fletcher gets hurt. How Jeffrey handles the situation makes a lively story. The plot in *Prince of the Double Axe* is more complicated, but it, too, involves a problem. Here the problem is a struggle for freedom. All the events that follow the capture of Lycus, Skira, and Tirus lead toward their eventual escape. Those events make up the plot.

Setting The setting is the place and time in which the events in a story occur. In a good novel, setting is integral to the story. That means the plot could not have occurred in the same way anywhere else or at any other time. *Prince of the Double Axe* is historical fiction that must take place in ancient Crete and Egypt.

GLOSSARY

Vocabulary from your selections

a mi a ble (ā′mē ə bəl), having a good-
natured and friendly disposition; pleasant
and agreeable: *She is an amiable girl who
gets along with most people. adj.*

bier (bir), a movable stand or framework on
which a coffin or dead body is placed
before burial. *n.*

bran dish (bran′dish), wave or shake in a
threatening manner: *The knight brandished
his sword at his enemy. v.*

brig and (brig′ənd), person who robs
travelers on the road, especially one of a
gang of robbers in mountain or forest
regions; robber; bandit. *n.*

chol er a (kol′ər ə), an acute, infectious
disease of the stomach and intestines,
characterized by vomiting, cramps, and
diarrhea. *n.*

con coct (kon kokt′), prepare; make up: *He
concocted a drink made of grape juice and
ginger ale. They concocted an excuse for
being late to school. v.*

con coc tion (kon kok′shən), **1** a preparing
or making up: *The concoction of the milk
shake took several minutes.* **2** thing
concocted. *n.*

daw dle (dô′dl), waste time; idle; loiter: *Don't
dawdle so long over your work. I dawdled
the afternoon away. v.*

ed dy (ed′ē), move against the main current
in a whirling motion; whirl: *The water
eddied out of the sink. v.,* **ed died,
ed dy ing.**

concoction—The
chocolate sundae was
a magnificent
concoction.

fam ished (fam′isht), very hungry; starving: *We were famished after not eating anything for ten hours. adj.*

gape (gāp), **1** open the mouth wide; yawn. **2** stare with the mouth open: *The crowd gaped at the tricks performed by the tightrope walkers. v.,* **gaped, gap ing.**

gush (gush), rush out suddenly; pour out: *Oil gushed from the new well. v.*

har ry (har′ē), keep troubling; worry; torment: *Fear of losing her voice harried the ailing opera singer. v.,* **har ried, har ry ing.**

haugh ty (hô′tē), **1** too proud of oneself and too scornful of others: *A haughty person is often unpopular.* **2** showing too great pride of oneself and scorn for others: *a haughty glance, haughty words. adj.,* **haugh ti er, haugh ti est.**

heal (hēl), **1** make whole, sound, or well; bring back to health; cure. **2** become whole or sound; get well; return to health; be cured: *My cut finger healed in a few days. v.* **heal′er,** *n.*

Hin du (hin′dü), **1** person born or living in India. **2** of the Hindus, their language, or their religion. **3** person who believes in Hinduism. 1,3 *n., pl.* **Hin dus;** 2 *adj.*

ho mog e nize (hə moj′ə nīz), make similar or the same in kind. In homogenized milk the fat is distributed evenly throughout the milk and does not rise to the top in the form of cream. *v.,* **ho mog e nized, ho mog e niz ing.**

im mac u late (i mak′yə lit), **1** without a spot or stain; absolutely clean: *The newly washed shirts were immaculate.* **2** without sin; pure. *adj.*

jet ty (jet′ē), **1** structure of stones or wooden piles projecting out from the shore to break the force of a current or waves; breakwater. **2** a landing place; pier. *n., pl.* **jet ties.**

lan guid (lang′gwid), **1** feeling weak; without energy; drooping: *A hot, sticky day makes a person languid.* **2** without interest or enthusiasm; indifferent: *The lazy child felt too languid to do anything. adj.*

a hat	oi oil
ā age	ou out
ä far	u cup
e let	ù put
ē equal	ü rule
ėr term	
i it	ch child
ī ice	ng long
o hot	sh she
ō open	th thin
ô order	ᴛʜ then
	zh measure

ə = {
  a in about
  e in taken
  i in pencil
  o in lemon
  u in circus
}

languid (def. 1)

lep·ro·sy (lep′rə sē), disease caused by certain rod-shaped bacteria that attack the skin and nerves, causing lumps or spots which may become ulcers; Hansen's disease. If not treated, the injury to the nerves results in numbness, paralysis, and deformity. *n.*

louse (lous), **1** a small, wingless insect that infests the hair or skin of people and animals and sucks their blood. **2 louse up,** SLANG. spoil; get (something) all confused or in a mess: *louse up a deal.* 1 *n., pl.* **lice;** 2 *v.,* **loused, lous·ing.**

lum·ber (lum′bər), move along heavily and noisily; roll along with difficulty: *The old truck lumbered down the road. v.*

moor (mur), **1** put or keep (a ship, etc.) in place by means of ropes or chains fastened to the shore or to anchors. **2** fix firmly; secure. **3** tie down or anchor a ship. *v.*

moor·ings (mur′ingz), **1** ropes, cables, or anchors by which a ship is fastened. **2** place where a ship is moored. *n. pl.* Also **moor·ing.**

pas·sive (pas′iv), not resisting; yielding or submitting to the will of another: *The children gave passive obedience to their strict parents. adj.*

prow (prou), the front part of a ship or boat; bow. *n.*

quail (kwāl), be afraid; lose courage; shrink back in fear: *quail at the sight of a rattlesnake. v.*

quay (kē), a solid landing place for ships, often built of stone. *n.*

quay

ran·sack (ran′sak), **1** search thoroughly through: *A thief ransacked the house for jewelry.* **2** rob; plunder: *The invading army ransacked the city and carried off its treasure. v.*

rend (rend), **1** pull apart violently; tear: *Wolves will rend a lamb in pieces.* **2** split: *Lightning rent the tree. v.,* **rent, rend·ing.**

rite (rīt), a solemn ceremony. Most churches have rites for baptism, marriage, and burial. Secret societies have their special rites. *n.*

sa cred (sā′krid), **1** belonging to or dedicated to God; holy: *a sacred building.* **2** connected with religion; religious: *sacred writings, sacred music. adj.*

slick er (slik′ər), a long, loose, waterproof coat, a raincoat, made of oilskin or the like. *n.*

sluice (slüs), **1** structure with a gate for holding back or controlling the water of a canal, river, or lake. **2** flush or cleanse with a rush of water; pour or throw water over. **1** *n.,* **2** *v.,* **sluiced, sluic ing.**

sop (sop), **1** dip or soak: *to sop bread in milk.* **2** take up (water, etc.); wipe; mop: *Please sop up that water with a cloth. v.,* **sopped, sop ping.**

spire (spīr), **1** the top part of a tower or steeple that narrows to a point. **2** anything tapering and pointed: *The sunset shone on the rocky spires of the mountains. n.*

spon sor (spon′sər), **1** person or group that endorses, supports, or is responsible for a person or thing: *the sponsor of a law, the sponsor of a student applying for a scholarship.* **2** act as sponsor. **1** *n.,* **2** *v.*

staff (staf), a stick, pole, or rod used as a support, as an emblem of office, as a weapon, etc.: *The flag hangs on a staff. The woman leaned on her staff. n., pl.* **staves** or **staffs.**

tread (tred), **1** set the feet on; walk on or through; step on: *tread the streets* **2** act or sound of treading: *We heard the tread of marching feet.* **1** *v.,* **trod, trod den** or **trod, tread ing; 2** *n.*

ur gent (ėr′jənt), demanding immediate action or attention; pressing; important: *an urgent duty, an urgent message. adj.*

vague (vāg), not definite; not clear; not distinct: *In a fog everything looks vague. His vague statement confused them. adj.,* **va guer, va guest. —vague′ly,** *adv.*

yon (yon), OLD USE. yonder. *adj., adv.*

yon der (yon′dər), **1** within sight, but not near; over there: *The sky is getting black yonder in the west.* **2** being within sight, but not near; situated over there: *On yonder hill stands a ruined castle.* **1** *adv.,* **2** *adj.*

a hat	**oi** oil
ā age	**ou** out
ä far	**u** cup
e let	**u̇** put
ē equal	**ü** rule
ėr term	
i it	**ch** child
ī ice	**ng** long
o hot	**sh** she
ō open	**th** thin
ô order	**ᴛʜ** then
	zh measure

ə = {
a in about
e in taken
i in pencil
o in lemon
u in circus
}

spire (def. 1)

staff—staff for a flag

Text
Page 7: "Emergency!" from *The Revenge of the Incredible Dr. Rancid and His Youthful Assistant, Jeffrey* by Ellen Conford. Copyright © 1980 by Ellen Conford. By permission of Little, Brown and Company.
Page 26: "Barbara Frietchie" by John Greenleaf Whittier, 1864.
Page 30: From *The Gold Coin* by Alma Flor Ada. Text copyright © 1991 by Alma Flor Ada. Illustrations copyright © 1991 by Neil Waldman. Reprinted by permission of Atheneum Publishers, an imprint of Macmillan Publishing Company.
Page 46: "Ideas Are All Around Us" by Alma Flor Ada. Copyright © 1991 by Alma Flor Ada.
Page 51: "Love Until It Hurts" from *Mother Teresa, Sister to the Poor* by Patricia Reilly Giff. Copyright © 1986 by Patricia Reilly Giff. Used by permission of Viking Penguin, a division of Penguin Books USA Inc.
Page 62: "A Message of Love" by Patricia Reilly Giff. Copyright © 1991 by Patricia Reilly Giff.
Page 67: *Prince of the Double Axe* by Madeleine Polland. Copyright © 1976 by Madeleine Polland. Reprinted by permission of HarperCollins *Publishers*.

Artists
Illustrations owned and copyrighted by the illustrator.
Cover: Ron Villani
Pages 1–5: Ron Villani
Pages 6–24, 135: Jack Davis
Pages 27, 29: Peter Sis
Pages 30–45, 49, 135: Neil Waldman
Pages 66–130, 135: John Martinez
Pages 136, 138, 140, 144: Ron Villani

Photographs
Page 5: Pablo Bartholomew/Gamma-Liaison
Page 46: Courtesy of Alma Flor Ada
Page 50: Steve Liss/Gamma-Liaison
Page 53: C. LeRoy/Gamma-Liaison
Page 54: J. C. Francolon/Gamma-Liaison
Page 56: Pablo Bartholomew/Gamma-Liaison
Page 61: Susan Greenwood/Gamma-Liaison
Page 62: Courtesy of Patricia Reilly Giff
Page 63: AP/Wide World Photos
Page 64: Laurent Maous/Gamma-Liaison
Page 65: Pablo Bartholomew/Gamma-Liaison
Page 135 (top right): Steve Liss/Gamma-Liaison
Page 142: Dorka Raynor
Page 143 top: Salisbury Cathedral, Courtesy of the National Monuments Record
Unless otherwise acknowledged, all photographs are the property of ScottForesman.

Glossary
The contents of the Glossary entries in this book have been adapted from *Scott, Foresman Intermediate Dictionary*, Copyright © 1988 by Scott, Foresman and Company, and *Scott, Foresman Advanced Dictionary*, Copyright © 1988 by Scott, Foresman and Company.